# HOME BELOW HELL'S CANYON

# Home Below Hell's Canyon

GRACE JORDAN

UNIVERSITY OF NEBRASKA PRESS • Lincoln

Manufactured in the United States of America
Library of Congress Catalog card number 54-6332
International Standard Book Number 0-8032-5107-6

*First Bison Book printing: October, 1962*
*Most recent printing shown by first digit below:*

*6 7 8 9 10*

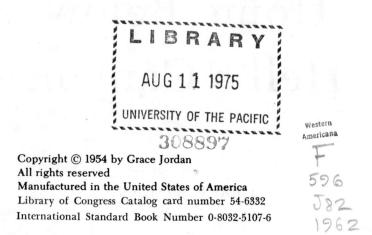

*Bison Book edition reprinted by arrangement with the author from the edition published by Thomas Y. Crowell Company*

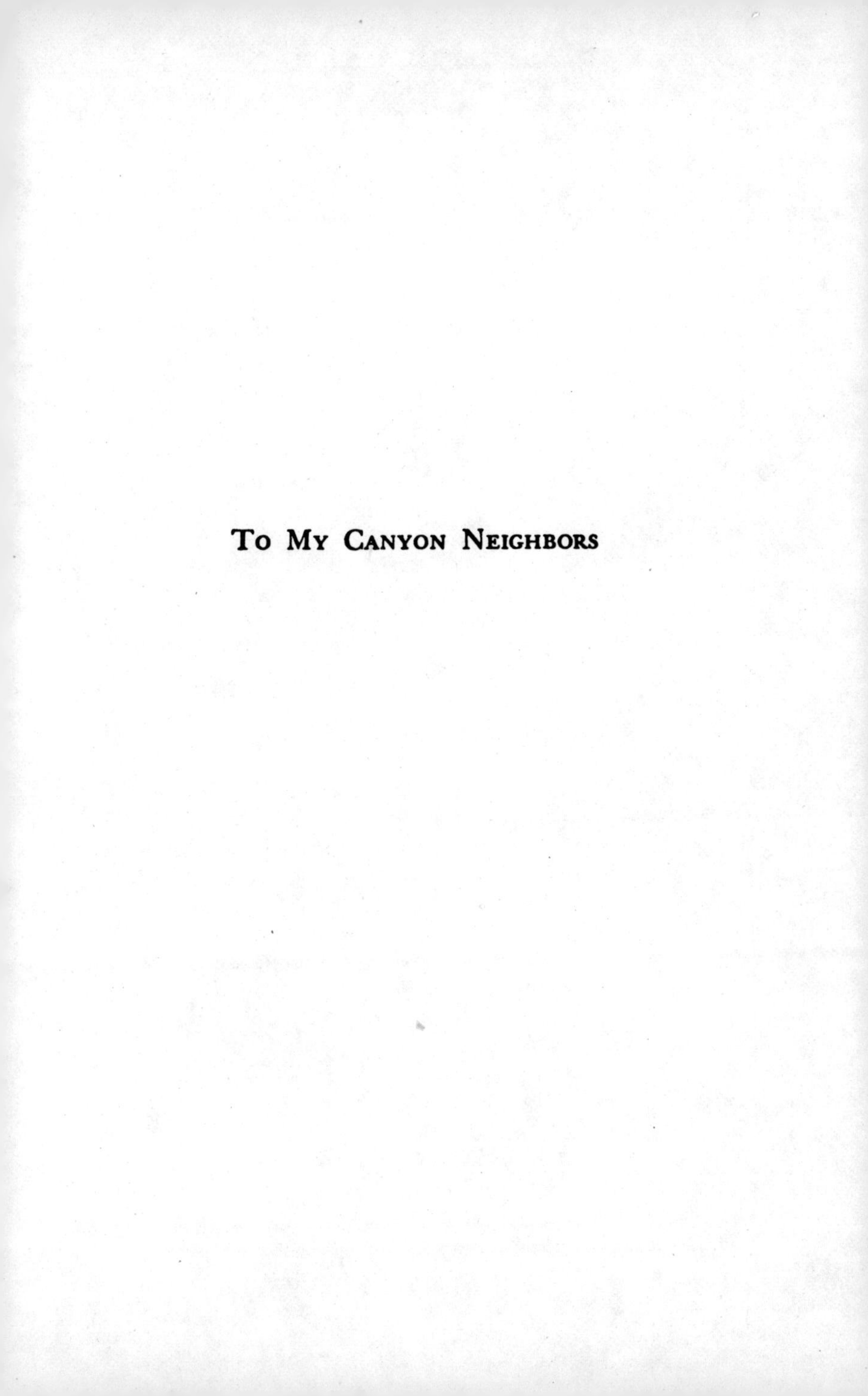

To My Canyon Neighbors

# *Author's Note*

The following account tells of the years that we spent on a sheep ranch in the Snake River canyon in middle Idaho. Place names are factual, though the time sequence has occasionally been altered for better story telling. Names of incidental characters have in a few instances been changed; but those people described as our neighbors were truly such, and life without them would have been harder and surely less delightful.

For help in establishing forgotten facts, I am indebted to Ellen Edgington and Page Hosmer, who returned old letters to me; and to Patsy, Joe, and Steve Jordan for the use of their diaries.

GRACE JORDAN

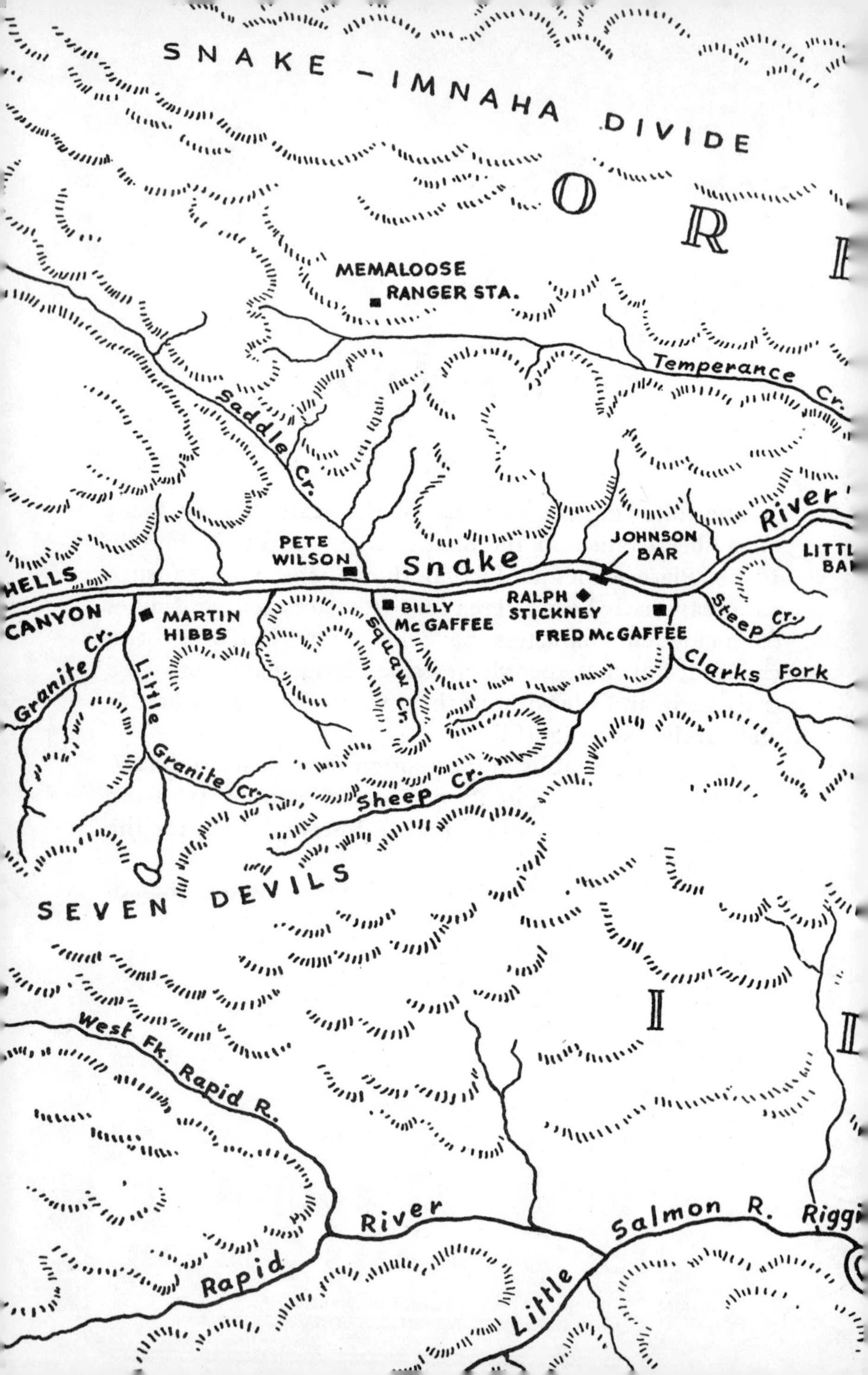

SNAKE - IMNAHA DIVIDE

O R

MEMALOOSE
RANGER STA.

Temperance Cr.

Saddle Cr.

River

PETE
WILSON

Snake

JOHNSON
BAR

HELLS

CANYON

MARTIN
HIBBS

BILLY
McGAFFEE

RALPH
STICKNEY

FRED McGAFFEE

Steep Cr.

Clarks Fork

Granite Cr.

Little Granite Cr.

Squaw Cr.

Sheep Cr.

SEVEN DEVILS

I

West Fk. Rapid R.

River

Rapid

Salmon R.

Little

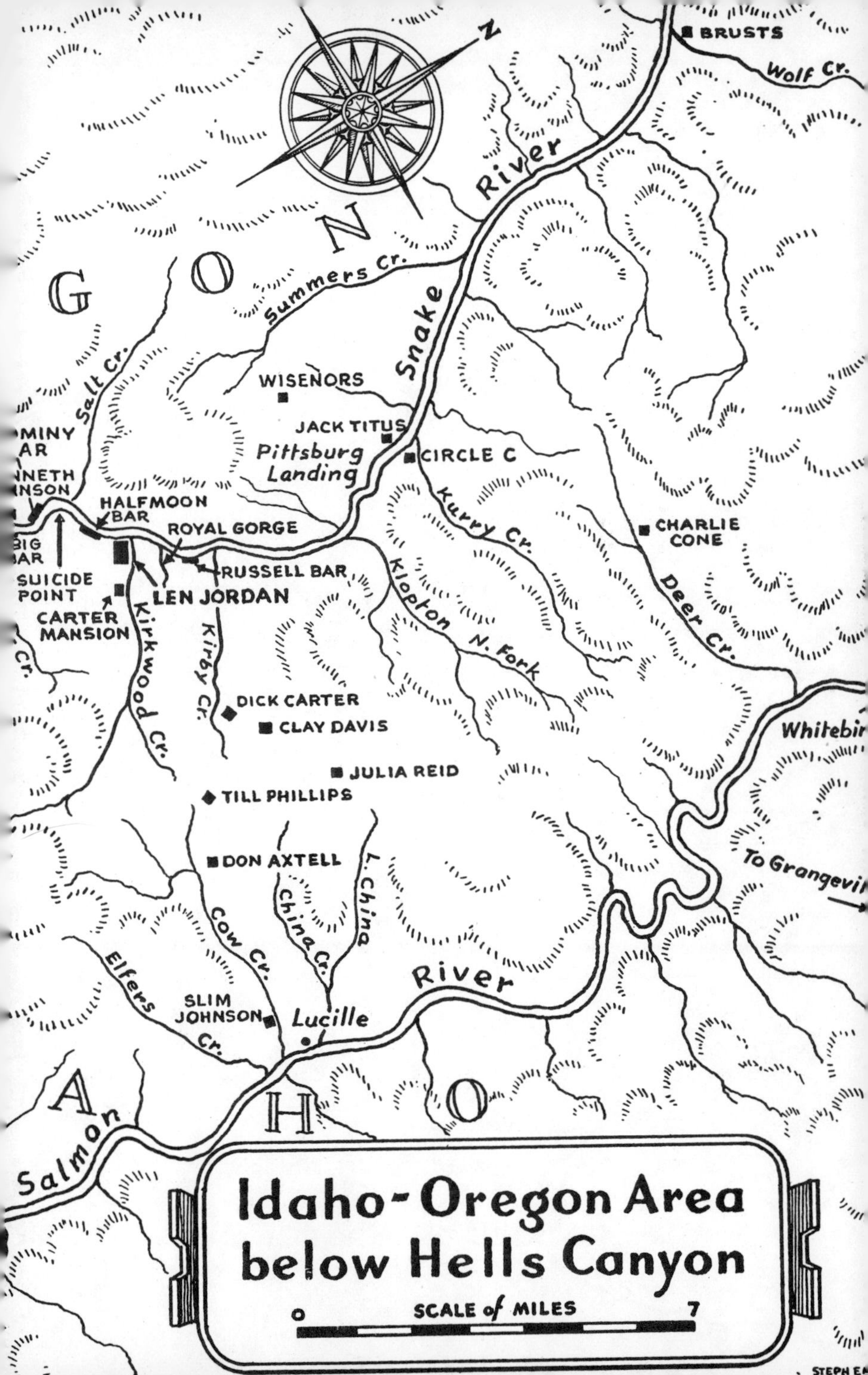

N
BRUSTS
Wolf Cr.
Snake River
G O N
Summers Cr.
Salt Cr.
WISENORS
JACK TITUS
Pittsburg Landing
CIRCLE C
HALFMOON BAR
ROYAL GORGE
RUSSELL BAR
SUICIDE POINT
LEN JORDAN
CARTER MANSION
Kurry Cr.
Klopton
N. Fork
CHARLIE CONE
Deer Cr.
Kirkwood Cr.
Kirby Cr.
DICK CARTER
CLAY DAVIS
JULIA REID
TILL PHILLIPS
Whitebir
To Grangevi
DON AXTELL
L. China
China Cr.
Cow Cr.
Elfers Cr.
River
SLIM JOHNSON
Lucille
A H O
Salmon
Idaho-Oregon Area below Hells Canyon
SCALE of MILES
0
7

# 1

AT FIVE-THIRTY, THAT MARCH MORNING, IT WAS STILL dark and quiet and the least bit cold along Snake River Avenue, as we transferred from taxi to dock, but in the warehouse of the Snake River Navigation Company of Lewiston there was activity and light. Captain Brewrink of the packet *Chief Joseph,* a lean, unhurried six-footer, relieved us of our hand luggage and gave us cheerful news. "Unless something happens," he said, "we can make Kirkwood tonight, say sixteen hours from now—that is, if there's moonlight."

The *Chief* lay rocking on the dark breast of the Snake, and we who picked our way down the gangplank together were five: my husband's father, two children, I, and the baby in my arms.

Grandpa nodded and smiled. He was a solid man of solid counsel, who never asked idle questions, and he already knew a great deal about the eighty-six miles of white water that tumbled between Kirkwood Bar, our destination, and the Lewiston, Idaho, boat dock. He had known and lived in the adjacent country for thirty years.

Thinking of the long hours ahead of us, I was thankful for the big lunch hamper I had brought. It held fruit, sandwiches, cheese, hard-boiled eggs, cookies and chocolate bars, and before leaving the hotel I had been able to buy three quarts of milk for the children. Grandpa and I would have to drink river water.

The *Chief* was not provisioned, and it had no berths. The captain and his helper carried big lunchboxes, thermos coffee, and their own sleeping bags; passengers could do likewise. But the children and I had already made a long train and bus trip before reaching Lewiston, and we possessed no bedding. I could not imagine how we would spend the night if the *Chief* had too many stops to make or if clouds blotted out the moon. The boat had no lights except kerosene lanterns—lights were useless for running since they only made the water opaque.

Kirkwood Bar was the sheep ranch which my husband and I, with a partner named Dick Maxwell, were buying. It lay in the Snake gorge, on the Idaho side, just below Hell's Canyon, that deepest scar on North America's face, through which the river is not navigable and where even foot travel stops. The business arrangements had been completed while I was with my parents, a day's journey west of Lewiston; and though I knew something of sheep ranches, I had never seen one in the shadow of an impassable canyon.

It was spring 1933, and the financial shaking of the past three years had jolted the Jordans badly. In those years we had abandoned running our own stock and had managed for another stockman, sometimes doing on wages of less than a hundred dollars a month plus our living, and I longed to get where we could operate again for ourselves, regardless of any physical hardship such ownership might involve. I was not disturbed by the isolation one must expect at Kirkwood and the two children were almost as eager as I to reach the new place their father had described in his letters. They had seen him but once in the last six months, for he had been at the ranch since purchase was completed, carrying on in a bachelor atmosphere.

Patsy was a sturdy six, with a straight Saxon bob and candid blue eyes above enduring freckles. Everything interested her to an extreme degree. Joe, at three and a half, was faintly olive skinned, quiet, but neither passive nor defenseless. Neither of them was objectionably self-important, for we had been surrounded a great deal by hired help or had stayed with other people. Children living thus must learn that everybody has his own preferences, and these must be observed.

Steve, seven months old, had big eyes and long lashes, and one very effective tool, a wide smile. That smile had sufficed all of yesterday, on the train to Pendleton, where Grandpa joined us, and even through the long bus hours to Lewiston on the Snake.

In Lewiston, where Joe had shared his grandfather's room, we had only a short night's sleep. Before daylight we were dressed and packed so as to have breakfast and be at the dock for the six o'clock departure of the boat, which made the canyon run only once a week. Breakfast did not benefit Steve much, for he was only half weaned, and the new sounds and faces in the cafe had distracted him from his cereal.

Our lunch hamper had been packed for thirty-six hours ahead of time, since I had known there might be no place or time enroute to buy suitable food. It was unthinkable to miss the weekly boat, and for two reasons. In the first place I was almost out of money; and in the second, the children and I had nowhere else to go. The failure of our bank a week before had wiped out my checking account, and I had, literally, only the money in my purse.

For traveling expenses, my mother had been able to secure twenty dollars in "hard" money for me; and a friend, appearing opportunely, had loaned me a five dollar bill. It looked as if we would make it to Kirkwood, where coin would buy practically nothing, but we might make it by only a neck. With gratitude I remembered that Grandpa had picked up the dinner check last night, and paid for breakfast this morning; but that was Grandpa's way.

In the body of the boat we found seats on the benches running along two sides of the single compartment back of the pilothouse and serving as a step-down from the little deck. On the dock side, the canvases were rolled to admit freight and passengers. Through the slits on the other side I could get glimpses of the river as the light increased.

Here the Snake was broad and smooth, flowing down from between purple hills on the south, hills with vegetation at the water's edge but fairly bald above. On the opposite bank slumbered the little city of Clarkston, and farther down a bridge arched across between the two towns.

In the up-river coves a delicate fog floated, but beyond this and the bare hills unreality closed in, for there the stream made a bend, drawing a curtain on life above. On another trip I had been considerably above that bend, and I knew that the hills increased in steepness and that the arrogant Snake tore down between them in relentless power. But of the final barrier, Hell's Canyon, where neither boats nor men but only wild animals had penetrated, of that I knew merely the stories I had heard. And Kirkwood lay just this side.

Other passengers dropped down into the boat, and the children whispered cautiously to me, or went to consult Grandpa. They wore wool caps and jackets with their home-made coveralls, and boots suitable for rough ground—and rattlesnakes. At the hotel Grandpa had changed to a tweed jacket and wool shirt. He was a proud man, too proud to use a cane though he had been a little lame all his life; and the children knew they were never to speak about the metal piece that went up under his trouser leg. I had changed from skirt to trousers, and I wore boots with wool socks. My camel's-hair coat felt good against the damp breeze curling along the water.

Never having been on a boat before, the children were excited at the prospect of riding on water for a whole day, eating meals from a basket and being with Grandpa. They carried no toys nor pets. Lugging needless things was not our idea of common sense, and the children already comprehended this.

Freight piled in until a mountain of it lay between the pilothouse and the little coal stove at our end. The passenger area had disappeared, but this did not matter since the freight itself made good seating. The *Chief* gave gently with each added bale and box, merely settling a bit deeper into the greenish Snake.

Joe whispered in my ear.

"As soon as the boat starts," I answered. "It's the little door you see behind me. Grandpa will go with you."

"Mother?"

"Yes?"

"When will it be lunch? I think Grandpa's awfully hungry."

"We've just had breakfast! Grandpa isn't hungry, he's thinking. In about two hours you can have a sandwich and some milk, but it won't really be lunch until twelve." Then I showed him my wrist watch and how far the little hand must travel until he could eat.

"Will Cooky be there to see me when I get off the boat?"

"Cooky? Oh yes, the little puppy Daddy wrote about, and he asked you to send a name for it. No, I think Cooky will be asleep with his mother, but you can play with him tomorrow, I'm sure."

"Do I have to take a nap today, Mother?"

I smiled. "Do you see any place to take one?"

Joe grinned with delight.

Among our fellow travelers were stockmen, bronzed and wrinkled by summer glare; two odd females going up to cook somewhere; and a man in correct gray who might be a loan-company representative. A dim little gnome that I took for a prospector sat on a sack of flour and rolled a cigarette nervously. He glanced at nobody and nothing, as if rocks were the only things that mattered.

Patsy stole a look at me to see if I too found him amusing, her eyes twinkling above her round cheeks.

No other child came aboard, but we gave this no thought. We did not realize that we were moving into a region of no children, a land of single men, middle-aged widows, and married couples who were either childless or boarded their children in towns where there were schools.

Captain Brewrink took a last look around the warehouse, then tossed in the mailbags. The gangplank was pulled and the *Chief* gave a sharp lurch. Patsy and Joe shot me anxious looks, but Grandpa quieted them with a gentle pressure.

Here we go, I thought. I was rather glad my mother could not see us now. Yesterday morning, as we waited for the taxi to take us to the depot, she had said: "Some day you'll come out of that canyon with your health gone and the children queer." She had whispered the word "queer."

Since I had already said everything there was to say I only shook my head.

"It's wicked to throw away your life like that," she insisted.

"But, Mother, when you first went to the wheat country in eastern Oregon, as a young doctor's wife, you found things rough, too."

"But we had a church and a school—and *people!*"

"If it's loneliness you mean, Len and I know how to stand a good deal of that. I think we can do without church for a while; and I can teach the children."

"You can't teach them if you have men to cook for, and *all* your housework and washing, and a little baby to take care of. Then there's the river! And Len said there was a creek! The children will drown!"

"No. You have to teach children to stay away from such things. They've already learned that there are rules, and that rules have to be obeyed."

"But you've never lived in a place as bad as *this* one. Why are you always going to a *worse* place! Len could get a job here, teaching, or in business—"

"No," I said again. "We've found what we want—a sheep ranch where the range is good because it's inaccessible. And this is the right time; sheep can't go much lower. That's the way you're supposed to do it: buy 'em low, ride 'em up. But good range is absolutely necessary, and you take it where you can get it."

My father, gentle man, uttered not a word of protest and in parting he only pressed the baby's round cheek against his for the last time.

So now as we eased to the quickening motion of the *Chief*, the stevedore hurried down deck to loose the rolled curtains. Then somebody put coal in the stove and that was it! We were off.

I pulled my curtain a bit so I could get a peep of the river vista as it changed. In this smooth water the boat made fast time, and soon we were approaching the bend in the stream. The hills stood out more boldly now, and the cultivated bars began to pinch off. The sun was still invisible, but a sudden ray lanced through a high notch and smote the opposite hills. Impersonal and lofty, the sky glittered with promise and excitement.

Grandpa was explaining: "Not until the day warms up a bit. As we go farther up the river, the wind will drop. Then I'll take you both up on deck. Around at the stern—that's the back—we'll have the high wall to protect us." His statement was sufficient; Grandpa always kept promises.

At nine the children had sandwiches and milk, and at twelve we really went *into* the lunch basket. Grandpa loved cheese, and we had brought his favorite kind. He helped the children manage their oranges so as to get the least juice on face and clothes, and he peeled an orange for me. Stephen drank a little milk, wrinkling his nose because it was cold.

"There's an old fellow outside that hasn't anything to eat," Grandpa said. "Could we spare him a little?"

I thought, if we don't make it through tonight—

"I saw his shoe," Patsy said earnestly. "It has a hole, and he has a kind of dirty face, but maybe he can't help it."

"I think a mouse ate his shoe in the night," Joe added.

"Of course we can spare something," I said, ashamed of my reluctance. "Take him some meat sandwiches and some eggs. They're already peeled."

"A good thing they're peeled and wrapped in paper," Grandpa told the children, "because the old fellow's hands have come unwashed too!"

"I could go along and help you," Patsy offered.

"No," Grandpa said. "The water's too rough right now. It's hard even for me to keep my feet. The passengers will soon be coming in, I think."

They did come, but with the constant stops we were losing cargo fast, and there was now plenty of seating room inside. Smoke puffed from the stove, and one curtain had to be kept up but it was better to be a little cold than not to see everything. Sometimes, after discharging groceries, or horseshoes or mail, Captain Brewrink looked in on us. He smiled but wasted few words.

Through the middle of the day a new twist in the canyon sometimes brought a deceitfully smooth stretch of water, and for a few moments the face of the sun. At such times Grandpa took the two children on deck. Once he assumed charge of the baby and I went up myself. I was there when we came abreast of the great inflow of the Salmon. Up this precipitous gorge, Chinese had mined for gold forty or fifty years before—they had mined and been massacred. Massacred by white men, so the story ran, men who searched in vain for the gold they thought the Chinese had cached. And ever since, someone was always returning secretly to renew the search.

We anchored at Eureka, where the little Imnaha River comes quarreling in and the ruins of a stone smelter stretch up the cliff. Here, on the sandbar, waited a party of people and horses. A weekly boat on the Snake cannot keep a tight schedule; these folks expected to wait and they had brought their lunch, built a fire and made coffee.

Some understanding soul, hearing that a woman with a baby was on board, passed in a quart jar of coffee. It was tepid but good and strong, mellowed with canned milk.

Shortly we were under way again, advancing between walls that rose in volcanic rims on the right and in disordered domes and pinnacles on the left. The Snake, Grandpa explained to me, ran in a colossal fault here, and that was why the two walls were unlike.

Now the river was flinging itself between its pillars with special frenzy, and the little bars and prospector stops fell away. For miles the walls rose straight, never far apart, and the deep voice of the engines beat back and forth, exciting and disturbing.

Suddenly the canyon opened for a constricted ranch with weathered buildings, but the bit of field above the rocky terrace was lush with green. Grandpa pointed to the field. "The winters here are mild," he said contentedly. "In the main, of course. Mild winters, no roads reaching in. That's why it's a great stock country."

The United States Forest range, as I already knew, made it possible for the owner of a very few acres of hay land to run thousands of sheep or cattle. The government range, if used continuously and properly by the land owner or his tenant, came to "belong" to the deeded land, and could be transferred to a new owner if the land were sold. Because of such Forest "rights," the land thus came to have a value far exceeding what it actually produced, but a stockman would raise and jealously preserve every possible ton of hay on his arable acres as a bulwark against the occasional bitter winter when stock could not survive on range grass alone.

The separate plots to which we had actual title totaled less than a thousand acres, yet the range they "controlled" was over seventeen thousand acres in extent, lying for ten miles along the river and climbing in places to the Salmon-Snake divide.

This range was very steep—that was why the Forest Service assigned it to sheep rather than to cattle—and some of it not usable at all, but what was used must be used under the direction of the Forest organization, and a fee paid for each head of stock grazed.

Our summer range, which would be assigned us in higher, cooler country, was smoother than the tilted home acres and would have to be reached by "trailing" the sheep a hundred miles.

Day was gradually wearing away, but we were shipping so much water now that the decks were constantly slippery, and sometimes a wave burst in on the floor of the boat. After ten hours the engine vibration was penetrating my very bones, and it was a strain to talk above the throb and pound. Only a few passengers remained with us, and there was nothing to do but endure as best we could.

At five we had a last cold snack and settled down for the final wait. Though the river had taken on the color of smoke, the sky above the rims was pale and clear, and if it stayed this way the moon would show and the *Chief* could keep on after nightfall. As we drove through the increasing dusk I realized that if the walls on both sides dropped as sheerly below the water as they rose above it we would be in bad case to ram them in the gloom.

Neither Grandpa nor I questioned the captain as to when we would reach Kirkwood, since he could answer in miles only; the time naturally increased with each mail stop. It was dark when we passed Wolf Creek and its minute glimmer of light. The children were too weary to hold themselves on the benches any longer, or to stand by Grandpa's knees. They tried lying on a pile of flour, but when this was unloaded they lost this quite unyielding couch. After that they sat on the floor boards, dimly watching the dark bilge circulating a few inches beneath. In time they dropped asleep in painful postures against Grandpa's legs or mine, until they went limp and collapsed. All I could do, as I held the sleeping baby, was to see that the other children did not roll against the stove.

Whenever I asked, Grandpa scooped me a drink of river water. Perhaps it had germs, but it tasted wet. Our lunch basket held nothing now but drying scraps, and the milk was long since gone. All we really wanted was to get to the end of our journey.

Captain Brewrink looked neither tired nor worried. He had told us he could determine where we were by the outline of the cliffs against the sky and from that he knew where the channel should be. Whenever the *V* of the gorge caught the moon, he could actually see the rapids. For fifteen years or more Captain Brewrink had been running the river with a great record for safety, so when the *Chief* bumped something with an alarming recoil, I reminded myself sternly that my husband would never have told us to board this boat if it would not get us to him in safe condition.

Suddenly our speed slackened, and we seemed to be standing in to shore.

"This is it, I guess," Grandpa exclaimed cheerfully, "but don't move until I make sure."

No, it wasn't Kirkwood. It was Circle-C on the Idaho side, and there were lights on the Oregon side too. Over there was Pittsburg ranch. Both sets of lights seemed far away, with a world of blackness between. Above the ebony of the gorge, the yellow moon sailed in a cold indigo sea. The gleam of the moon on the spray, where the river licked at a hidden reef, was cold too as we settled back for another hour of muscle cramps and stomach ache.

The baby waked and cried. He went on crying hopelessly, clutching my face, imploring consolation. All day he had been good, all day yesterday too. Now he was slept out, poor thing. The smoke stung my eyes and his; my bones ached, my arms cried. Another hour to go.

"Kirkwood in five minutes!"

At this sound, Grandpa was on his feet, and began grouping the bags, and rousing the children. Until they found me, their eyes were round and frantic. Then they shook off sleep and came alive.

"Will Daddy be there when we get off this boat?" Patsy cried as she pushed her yellow hair out of her eyes and smoothed her wrinkled clothes.

Joe swayed on wobbly legs. "Will we ride horses?" he piped.

"Put on your things and sit on the bench out of the way," I said, feeling pretty excited myself.

"It's no use going up on that slippery deck until they come to help us," Grandpa said sensibly. "We might skid into the river and nobody would miss us!"

Patsy giggled at such absurdity, hugging herself with rapture.

The engines slowed, and from under the hull came the authoritative gurgle we had already heard thirty times. The *Chief* rocked sideways, there was a stiff jolt, then silence. We sat down hard. What on earth had happened! Nothing, evidently, for now we heard the plank going out, and immediately a man's voice and the clump of heavy shoes along the deck.

The curtains beyond the swinging lantern parted.

"Daddy!"

"Hello, everybody!" My husband jumped down into the boat and went to take his father's hand. "How are you, sir! You got them here, didn't you!"

Len was gathering Patsy and Joe into his arms in one big hug, standing so close I could feel his warmth, and get the smell of wool, leather and tobacco that went with him. He stood six feet tall, blue eyed, very solid, with the kind of voice that says, "You don't have to worry any more."

Joe was asking, "Daddy, is Cooky here?" but my husband had turned to me. I felt his lips. "Hello, honey," he said quietly. "You're here at last!" He took the baby from me. "I'll carry this rascal. Are you pretty tired?"

Wrenched from uneasy sleep, Steve began to bellow.

"Here, here," his father cried gaily. "None of that! Don't you know you're home now!"

"He's worn out," I said.

"Worn out! With sleeping in somebody's arms! Well, let's get moving. The welcoming committee awaits on the sand."

With his free hand Len scooped up everything he could carry; Grandpa guided the children; I brought the lunch hamper and my portable typewriter.

Huddled in the bright moonlight on the bar were men and mules. They clustered about a lighted lantern that looked a little foolish in competition with the moon. I could see the walls of the canyon, their jagged combs, and the spectacular jet shadows that pocked their stony sides. But this was no time for the appreciation of beauty.

Dick Maxwell, our partner, came forward. I had seen

him but once before, yet his thin face and spare frame were unmistakable. We shook hands. I was introduced to Uncle Jimmy, a majestic little man with a breast-long beard—he was the temporary ranch cook, I knew. Then there was a packer, lambing helpers that had already arrived, and a neighbor.

"Take the folks right up," Dick said hospitably. "I'll bring the bags and whatever freight has to be moved tonight."

Dick meant that the others would do it. He did not pack. He had never worked in the canyon, or run sheep, and had come into the partnership only as an investor, not to stay at the ranch or "make a hand." But this he had now decided to do. Unmarried, previously a successful businessman in a small town, his family ties were only those of numerous relatives. One of these was a brother-in-law, from whom we were buying the ranch. Another was his unmarried sister Anna, who had reigned as housekeeper at Kirkwood for the several years that her nephew, Kenneth Johnson, had operated this outfit. All this relationship sounds complicated, but many canyon outfits are involved family affairs.

Kenneth Johnson, also a bachelor, was now running the Temperance Creek ranch, four miles farther up the river and on the Oregon side; and his aunt, Anna, had moved there with him.

"Dick's sister is up at the house," Len said, as if this explained itself.

"How far is the house?" I asked.

"Only a step," my husband said easily. "Here, you kids, follow me. If there's a rattler in the alfalfa, I'll walk on him first." He picked up a lantern and we set off.

We followed along the edge of a narrow field with a

dramatic inky cliff at its back, and after we had walked the length of this field, I saw the cliff was breaking away and I could hear a shallower roar than that of the river.

"We cross the creek here," Len said. "You can't see the house because of the brush and trees along the creek. Watch the footlog, kids!"

Ascending from the crossing, we saw lighted windows close at hand, and soon we stood in a big kitchen. Anna Maxwell greeted us, and turned out to be much like her brother, except that her voice held more authority.

"So the boat made it through," she said pleasantly. "I told Len I'd stay until morning anyhow. I've got some bread and cake baked ahead; you'll have something to start with."

I was puzzled about her being here at all and responded inadequately, my husband thought.

"Anna's been on the go since early morning," he said. "At Temperance Creek they put her and her horse across the river at daylight, and she came down here alone. Over Suicide. Of course she just laughs about *that* trail. She sure has cleaned up our place!"

I looked about. In the big room there was a range with high warming oven and reservoir, a scarred woodbox and work table, a tall cabinet with glass doors, and a square dining table with the usual centerpiece composed of salt and pepper, catsup, sugar and canned milk. Against the wall behind the table sat a long, low chest, evidently used as a couch also, and there were unpainted chairs and boxes for additional seats. I was happy to see on the wall an old-fashioned telephone. On the stove a marbled blue teakettle was purring.

"How about something to eat?" Anna asked.

"I just want to get the children to bed," I said. Grandpa

declared he wasn't hungry, but if there was some coffee—

"There is! Still hot!" Anna was already getting it. "And now about beds. There's just the two bedrooms. Len and his father can take one, and you and the children the other. Dick and the men are all fixed up in the bunkhouse."

"But where will *you* sleep?" I asked.

"Oh, right here on the chest. There's plenty of bedding."

Anna was not to be argued with, and besides there seemed no other solution.

The bedrooms were mere cubicles, each containing a double bed and a table. One of them had an outside door. As Len helped me undress the children I exclaimed, "Why, you have sheets!"

"Oh sure! We have *four* sheets! They came with the ranch, but I think Anna has had them at Temperance Creek for safe keeping until you could get here."

Even before their shoes were off the children were nodding. So when Len had told me goodnight, I blew out the light and took off my clothes. It was necessary to blow out the light because there were no curtains. Then I opened the windows and leaned out against the night.

From the grass and budding orchard came a faint fragrance . . . this drooping shadow was a tree trying to come in my very window . . . that dark huddle must be the bunkhouse . . . and out there was the river. Its murmur came vaguely, but only because of the distance. There was certainly nothing vague about the Snake, and vague people would not clutter its canyon long, I thought.

I was filled with peace, for everything was right. We had made it; the children were whole, undamaged, asleep with their bright dreams. Tomorrow morning they would be plaguing me to get out and see everything. And I had arrived with three dollars to spare!

The floor was no longer rocking, and if I stood at the window much longer I knew I'd be asleep on my feet. I was here, and Len was here, just beyond that thin plasterboard partition.

# 2

THE MAGIC OF THAT MARCH MORNING AT KIRKWOOD is not hard to recreate, the dreaming light on field and river, and in contrast the stark wall opposite, down which the invisible sun was beginning to push a glittering saw-toothed line. Directly outside my west window lay a weedy area edged by straggling lilacs on one side and by ancient apple trees on the other, with the bunkhouse closing the rectangle. At the south end of this log building rose a stone chimney; at the other end the roof projected to make enough shelter for an anvil and a forge. A saddled horse stood tied to a hitching rack close to the anvil.

To the left and right the green alfalfa streamed away, bisected by the creek. It was the one tender bit of ordered life against all the rock and crag.

From the kitchen I could hear voices. My bobbed hair took but little time to comb, so I was dressed in five minutes. Anna and Grandpa looked up from their conversation as I came in. Anna said, "I thought you should sleep late this one morning. The men have all had breakfast and most of them took their lunches along. I'll be leaving too."

A few minutes later we went to watch her mount Dirty Face, a good enough beast with unfortunate markings. Uncle Jimmy emerged from the bunkhouse carrying a Bible with his finger between the pages, and Dick came too to tell his sister goodbye. As best I could I expressed my thanks to her for all she had done to put the ranch-house in order and give me a good start.

"Ring me any time," Anna invited, "if you're puzzled about something."

She rode off, through the apricot trees, past the English walnuts, and along the flume where clumps of wild peaches were growing. She would have to ride up over Suicide to reach Big Bar, where Kenneth would come by rowboat to meet her.

I went back to wake the children and prepare breakfast. Patsy and Joe were bubbling with impatience to get outside, and it seemed a good time to deliver a careful warning. I said: "Now the river's down there beyond the field. Neither of you is ever to go to the river unless you're with me or some other grown-up. Then, you remember, the creek is right out here beyond the house. If you fall into it, I don't think you'll drown, because it won't be over your head; and the brush would stop you from being swept very far. But *don't* fall in the creek. That would be silly!"

" 'Drown' means you get full of water and can't do what you want to," Patsy observed helpfully.

I went on: "The rattlesnakes aren't supposed to be out yet. But don't walk on rock piles, or in tall grass that you can't *see* into. Snakes are fond of rock piles and deep grass; and when it's very hot you'll find them in shady places by the water. Learn to be on the watch *all* the time when you're in snaky places."

For breakfast we had bacon, eggs and pancakes, but of course no fruit juice or fresh milk. On diluted canned milk the children simply gagged, but the previous winter they had learned to drink "Little Boy Coffee," which is what we called a mixture consisting of hot water with a little sugar and a good deal of canned milk. So now they had some of that. A milk cow had been bought, but she had not yet arrived. She would have to come up by boat at a time when the captain had room for her on the forward deck.

When we had finished eating there was plenty of morning left, and I could give Steve his first bath in three days. This refreshed him and made him merry. Then after he had been fed and played with he went back for another nap. Grandpa offered to babysit while reading a magazine, so the older children and I set out for a quick exploration of our new estate.

I especially wanted to see the Carter house, an empty dwelling up the creek which belonged to us, and about which Len had written. We set out at a brisk pace, up the trail toward a bushy green barrier where the walls of the creek pinched in as if they meant to close. To the left rose a terraced height falling back as it rose, with bands of grass between rocky outcrops, its top crowned with battlements against the sky. On the right Kirkwood Rock soared aloft, too sheer for anyone to climb far. We pushed between the irrigation flume and the right wall, and came out into a surprising little meadow, elliptical in shape with steep cliffs on both sides. A lone poplar grew by the water, and on the farther side I saw ruins of a small stone structure, perhaps a homesteader's crude cabin, or an old root cellar. Somebody had once lived in this green silence.

At the upper end of the meadow the walls pinched together much more formidably, so that a few yards of fence and a gate made of poles, barbed wire and some sheets of corrugated tin barred all stock from passing. Here Kirkwood Rock literally overhung, creating a shade so dense it seemed almost sinister.

Passing through the gate—to us it was now the "tin" gate—we climbed by gentle stages for a half mile, crossing the creek on stones several times. Suddenly we came upon the bleached skeleton of a mule or horse—we did not know which at the time—and it served later as a landmark. The children could say, "Mother, I went as far as the dead mule."

By this time the creek basin had widened, and topping a rise we found ourselves looking into a shoestring alfalfa field. Still no house, but we trotted on.

Suddenly there it stood, the Carter house, the sun drawing steam from its wet shakes, and the sumac and elderberry bushes pushing against its blank windows. As we scrambled across the creek to its cement-floored porch, the special virtues of this building became evident. Built of peeled logs set vertically on a foundation of rock and concrete, with metal strips over the chinking, the house had been designed to stand a hundred years. The big windows had screens, and behind the front door screen a frosted stag pranced upon the glass of the door.

The porch, alas, had begun to crumble under the hooves of inquisitive horses and deer; and we found the back porch in the same condition. Since both doors were locked, we climbed through a rear window. Inside were five plastered rooms which had obviously been lived in. But a dining table and chairs and other odd pieces of furniture were the only remaining evidence of the bootlegger who had built this honest house.

I knew the facts about Dick Carter and how, after he had been tried and served his time uncomplainingly, he had come back here for a little while. But then he had sold the place to our predecessor, who desired to round out his holdings, and now Carter lived on a big ranch on the divide above, a ranch which he ran as efficiently as he had erected this house and operated his hidden still.

Obviously this was the house that should stand on Kirkwood Bar. I wondered then, as did nearly everybody who saw it, how it could be moved. Some people even suggested sawing it in two and levering it through the jaws of the creek in sections. But for now, the children and I contented ourselves by renaming it "Carter Mansion." Then reluctantly we took ourselves away.

Lunch was not difficult. For fresh vegetables I found in the basement a supply of parsnips, potatoes, carrots, rutabagas, onions, and even some cabbage. A shelf of canned fruit had come with the ranch, and we had brought our own supply as well.

The baby waked from his nap and played happily on a blanket on the floor. After lunch Len came in from his circle of inspection and had time to help me rearrange our sleeping quarters. For ourselves we took the room with the outside door, and here we placed a cot for Patsy, and over the foot of our bed a small swinging bunk for the baby. By day it could be drawn up out of the way; at night it would be easy to reach.

We prepared the other room for Joe and Grandpa. There was also time to set up a washing machine Len had found in a used furniture shop in Lewiston. With great pride he had ordered it sent up the river.

I had never seen a machine like this. It had a long, low platform on steel legs, big enough not only for the giant washer but for two rinsing tubs, with a fixed crossbar to hold a second wringer. With its elaborate gears and large flywheel, it was an impressive sight when we placed it in the yard, by the irrigation ditch.

For supper we could have boiled mutton, and I found it easy to build a meal around this. At five o'clock Uncle Jimmy came in, wearing an official manner.

"I always make the graham gems for Mr. Maxwell," he stated. "He has to have them."

I nodded uncertainly.

The old gentleman's first move was to take out his dental plates. "I can't think with them in," he said smiling.

When the graham bread was in the iron pan, he went to the sourdough jug. "I'll make the hotcakes for breakfast—you've probably never handled sourdough. And I'll make the coffee *all* the time," he announced gently.

Sounds from the yard indicated that the supper crowd was arriving, large and hungry. The herders had a couple of dogs apiece, whose names I would come to know, and these were quarreling amiably now with Fannie, Queen, and Shiner, the home dogs. Fannie, a small, too-knowing brown creature, was having a rest just now, with little to do but look after Cooky, the only one of her puppies that had been saved. Queen was a much bigger, more solemn old girl, whose usefulness seemed about ended, but she also was about to add to the dog population. Neither Fannie nor Queen could claim shepherd blood, but this makes little difference in a sheep dog. A well-trained mongrel if loved and fed sufficiently often becomes invaluable.

Shiner, a mixed gray and white Australian shepherd who *looked* like a prize, was a dog of such weak character no herder wanted him around. He stole from camp boxes just to be stealing, when he was not even hungry, and his whitish eyes concealed all his thoughts.

Until supper was over, probably until several suppers were over, the Uncle Jimmy problem would have to wait. For after all he was seventy-eight years old, a lone man who also came with the ranch; and now I had arrived to threaten his tenure as cook and therefore his peace. At lunch he had suggested with dignity that he would say the blessing. It might have been months since he had been allowed to say one, though he read a chapter in his Bible every morning after breakfast, regardless of any delays this might cause. On the other hand he could curse with skill—so the boys said. Altogether a delightful old man, and when he spoke of Len I could tell from his tone that he loved him warmly.

For the present I must prevent Uncle Jimmy from holding the baby, who was fascinated by his beard; and Len might be able to think of something outside the house for him to do. He had stated that he wished to remain at Kirkwood only until spring ended, and I knew my husband would feel there was surely some simple solution to a minor problem like this, and that I should find it without hurting the feelings of a faithful old man.

Before supper we had found an additional table, so that even with me and the children, everyone could sit down at once. In his little green carriage Steve sat up beaming as he munched dry toast. Tomorrow we would unpack his high chair, and also screw a hook to the kitchen ceiling for his canvas jumper.

It was curiously peaceful to be again in a setting where meat, potatoes and gravy had honest dominion, and where pie was food, not something to indicate the end of a meal. My hungry men ate ravenously, leaving nothing; yet by eight o'clock the kitchen was empty, the dishes done, and all the dogs fed. The children were in their beds, the bunkhouse light was out.

The darkness of our narrow little bedroom closed us in. I recounted my morning to Len, after he had told me of his. Then I spoke of Carter Mansion.

"Not *Mansion,*" my husband reproved me. "*Mansion* is silly."

I was too drowsy to argue, knowing anyhow that I would call it whatever I liked, at least to myself.

The next morning, after all the help had gone outside, Grandpa said to me, "I swear I can't hold enough of Uncle Jimmy's coffee to get any good out of it. Can't *you* make the coffee?" And Dick Maxwell added, "I wish you would take over making my graham bread."

Len, studying his memoranda, did not hear this conversation. His mind was on three thousand ewes that were due to lamb in the next six weeks or so. I told the two men that I'd see what I could do. However, it was graham flour that really solved the problem. Dick's mention of it had given me an idea, and while Uncle Jimmy was reading his chapter in the bunkhouse that morning, I stirred up the sourdough jug myself. In place of half of the usual white flour I substituted graham, honestly believing it would improve the hotcakes; certainly I intended no harm.

The following morning, though I hurried to the kitchen, Uncle Jimmy was there ahead of me. When he poured out the hotcake dough, he saw that something unorthodox had happened to the jug. In the canyon, baking soda is a remedy for whatever is wrong, inside or outside the house. So Uncle Jimmy doubled the amount of soda he usually sprinkled on the dough. Now he heated the long grease-encrusted iron griddle until it smoked, then poured a flock of cakes. They rose puffy, fell a little. Uncle Jimmy turned them, then proudly bore the stack to the table while the griddle re-heated to smoking prime.

My husband seized a pair of cakes, and spread on butter and a flood of golden syrup while Uncle Jimmy self-consciously started a new batch to browning. But Len took one bite, chewed with a startled expression, and dashed for the door. The other men stared, then tasted with caution and managed to stay seated, but no one wanted a second helping. They rounded off breakfast with eggs and bacon, and left quickly.

Uncle Jimmy and I were alone. He drew himself erect, fingering his beard tremulously. "Mrs. Gordon," he said—he could never remember whether my name was Gordon or Jordan—"I don't know why you did it, but you've *ruined* the sourdough."

I made no explanations, and after this Uncle Jimmy came in the house only to eat, or to bring my *Time,* which he always removed from the mail for himself.

There were other things than cooking to mark those first weeks, new people to get used to, gardening, and washing *on the board* because the new washer had proved a dud. Grandpa shortly returned to his business affairs; Uncle Jimmy presently went to live with friends, out where there was more civilization; Kenneth Johnson called on business; and we had a Sunday visit from Earl Hibbs, who lived at Granite Creek, the last ranch up.

Earl and his father, Martin Hibbs, lived alone. Because of impassable rapids, the boat could not get to Granite Creek. And before the government trail was shot out of the cliffs along the river, the Hibbs men had been forced to ride up around the heads of the gorges that brought down Squaw, Sheep, Slippery and Myers Creeks whenever they wished to get to the Salmon River by our trail. Yet Martin Hibbs had lived at Granite Creek for more than thirty-five years, and had reared six children there. Now his wife had died and all of the children but Earl had gone away.

Shortly after Earl's neighborly visit, another canyonite, Jake Gaus, came to see us, and his stay was to be longer than a single night. Jake also lived alone, but he put in all his time at a copper mine up the river. He was German, with a heavy accent, and he made a virtue of doing things as laboriously as possible. He moved great burdens on his back, the men told me—logs to saw up for his little cookstove and timbers to shore his mine tunnels. An outsider provided the money and Jake the labor in the mine, but it appeared that the money was nearly exhausted. Accordingly Jake had decided to hire out, and he stopped Len on the trail one day to ask for work as a lambing hand.

In the course of their talk, Jake explained that he belonged to a religious faith whose Sabbath came on a different day each year. Moreover he did not know whether he ought to work on his Sabbath, or should stay in his cabin, which was papered with religious mottoes, and engage in prayer and contemplation.

"Lambs seem to come along any day of the week," Len said. "The ewes pay no attention to the Sabbath."

"Then I will write to headquarters and get light on the matter," Jake offered.

The light turned out favorably, and something was found for Jake to do. But now, with lambing over, he still needed money, and Len suggested that he should excavate an area under the south half of our house. This appeared to be the logical way to get more living space, which we sorely needed. And so Jake, whom I had seen only when he stopped at Kirkwood, on his long trudges in and out of the canyon, came to board with me.

Rugged as an ox, heavy featured, with cloudy eyes that actually missed nothing, he had hands that looked as if they could choke a man or a cougar. He was deaf, and while it is no great loss to miss some ranch table talk, Jake was denied *all* human communication. At meals, either in sheep camp or at the house, the men talked about him over his head, and perhaps he knew they did.

On his side of the barrier, he attended well to his own wants, reaching with long arms, but offering nothing to anyone else. Then too Jake had still one more social handicap: he was decidedly unscrubbed.

That first morning he began his task by removing the wooden bulkhead in the basement wall, and he asked only the simplest tools for his work. During the first day other men were around; it was a cool, soothing sort of day, and Jake ate in his usual solid silence.

On the second morning, however, every man had an errand elsewhere, and even my husband found he had a business trip to make across the divide that would keep him several days.

So the children and I were now alone with Jake. Beneath the floor I heard the hollow, regular thump of his pick, and occasionally a muffled bump against the boards. I remembered having heard Jake referred to as "crazy." The day had begun warm, and its growing sultriness added to my feeling that all was not well, but I kept the children close and tried to remain calm.

At twelve o'clock, prompt to the minute, Jake was sloshing his face with water on the kitchen porch. He walked in and seated himself at the table. Standing at the range,

I turned to nod at him, and discovered that though he had washed, he had not dressed, as it were, for dinner. From the waist up Jake was attired in a woolen unionsuit. At least the garment on his thick torso was made like underwear, though it was a dingy brown.

It looked to me as if my Rubicon had come to dinner. I might as well face it. So I began to speak loudly, gathering courage with the sound of my own voice: "Mr. Gaus, where's your shirt?"

His eyes flicked, showing he had heard me. In hard tones he said: "In the bunkhouse. Why?"

"You'll have to put it on!" I shouted.

"Why?"

I felt my neck prickle, but I could not retreat now. I thought to myself, if I turn my back he'll hurl a plate at me! So I said loudly and sternly, "I don't care what you wear when you're working, but you *cannot* eat at my table in your underwear, no matter how hot it is."

Jake rose, paused significantly, walked out, the children staring after him in alarm. I could not just stand there, so I began to dish out the food. The children came closer and whispered to me nervously.

In a few minutes Jake returned, clothed in a wrinkled shirt. He seated himself pompously. I set the food on and got the children into their chairs. After an interval I addressed Jake with some simple query, certainly nothing about underwear.

Solemnly he fixed his smoky eyes on me; then he opened up!

For a few seconds I could scarcely tell what he was talking about, the long words came so steadily and in such noble cadence. Then I realized that he was talking about religion. He spoke as from a lofty height, his thoughts rolling from peak to peak and glittering with such gems as *luminosity, refulgence, radiance,* and *brilliancy.* I had never before heard so many words bearing on the qualities of light. Jake ended with the statement that to him had been "vouchsafed" a divine radiance possessed by few men.

Since I could only reply by lifting my voice to its highest pitch, it seemed a little ridiculous to attempt a philosophical debate. So all during dinner my boarder dominated the conversation, if it could be called that, but a different expression had come upon his face. He was practically smiling!

With dinner over, he bowed himself out and finished his rest hour in the yard. On the rustic table there he found a tablet and pencil and began drawing pictures, which he showed to the children, who stood close to watch him. Then he recited for them little poems he must have learned as a boy in Germany. Joe and Patsy were fascinated by the guttural sounds and conscientious rhyme.

Supper came. Jake delivered another address as he ate, *in his shirt.* Then he bowed again and once more he went to the yard with the children. At bedtime I slipped a loaded pistol under my pillow and put all three youngsters to sleep in my room. If Jake comes fooling around, I decided, I'll threaten him first. If he keeps on coming I'll shoot. At his legs.

As the silence of night increased I began to realize that the gun idea was not very sound. Jake wouldn't hear me threaten him, and to shoot a man without warning, especially if he was only looking for matches or a drink of water, was certainly unsporting. So I unloaded the .38 and fell asleep with no trouble at all.

Until the cellar was finished, Jake talked to me at every possible opportunity. When I went to inspect his work, I found it done with meticulous care. One boulder still stuck out of the wall, and it had been necessary to shape the cellar shelving around it. Dynamite, Jake explained gravely, was out of the question; and besides the rock might extend back many feet. The new earth floor was smooth, the walls uniformly sloped, and the shelves exactly level.

When he was ready to leave for his mine, Jake came to say goodbye. He cocked his head and asked me a question: "Who cuts the children's hair?"

"I do."

"Then you're the second-best barber on Snake River."

Overcome by such praise, I stammered, "Who's the best?"

"I am!" Jake stated, "and I can give spinal adjustments too."

I did not pursue the matter of adjustments, and we parted warmly.

On its last run, the *Chief* brought us Brownie, a young Jersey cow, a beautiful creature. She must have found the trip very exciting, since it was her first boat ride, and in addition the *Chief* broke its propeller when it had almost reached Kirkwood. The captain lost his anchor overboard and the *Chief* drifted until dark. Then it was maneuvered into an eddy. Brownie was probably in a state of nerves by the time the equally nervous boatmen got her on shore. Here she was milked by one of the passengers, and remained on solid ground for the night. In the morning a neighbor coming our way offered to bring her on. Brownie was due to freshen in the fall and was giving little milk so we cherished every drop. The children had had no fresh milk to drink for nearly three months.

# 3

From ten in the morning until seven at night the canyon was baking hot, but our household was small. It was June now, and only Dick and a man to do the irrigating remained at the ranch. The sheep were enroute to summer range in the mountains to the east, three weeks of laborious and sometimes heart-breaking travel that crossed rivers and prairies, penetrated deep timber, and threaded farm land.

At intervals Len rushed home to see about the hay and to make a round of the range. Summer offered some slack time for studying the best use of our winter grass on the Forest. It was possible that the winter camps could be placed better, and the number of days assigned to each could be adjusted to get forage that was being missed. Such changes would reduce the chances of over-grazing, which Len held to be a major sin. The United States Forest Service, which administered the range and must okay the number of sheep grazed and the number of days they spent at each camp, would be interested in any improvements that he could work out.

There was land to which we held title that we were not farming. The Camack place, a homestead added to the ranch to make a complete unit, just as the Carter land had been added, had once been farmed. It was an hour and a half away though almost directly overhead. Perhaps it would pay to put this land into use again. Big Bar, four miles up the river, might produce two big crops of hay if fuller use was devised of the waters of tumbling Myers Creek, which had to be flumed around a sickening cliff, and the flume was always coming apart up there. There was also the Foust place, still higher than the Camack homestead, and we wondered if a crop on this dry land would pay for the labor and justify the struggle of packing farm machinery up and back by mule.

Still pondering these problems Len had returned to the two bands on summer range.

The Fourth of July came without firecrackers, but it brought two welcome guests, ladies! It had been two months since I had seen another woman. Dick's sister Anna Maxwell and Mrs. Jack Titus from Pittsburg ranch had phoned they would call. I had never met Celia Titus, but she had sent me a baby's bathtub, her baby now being twelve, an independent young man able to go out of the canyon alone for schooling.

Too, Celia had proved a wonderful phone contact. When I could make no one answer over the burdened private line to Whitebird, Celia could get results, either because of better phone batteries or because her speech was more impressive. She could hear better too, since she was closer to central. The first time that I sought to know how fast Len could get home from Grangeville, by car, horse, and perhaps on foot, Celia checked the places he might pass and relayed to me his latest position. It was unbelievable how cleverly she had done this.

The ladies arrived well before lunch, Celia a little curious probably. The Tituses were ranchers of long standing, and Celia's mother and her unmarried brothers, the Wisenors, still ranched above Pittsburg on the Snake-Imnaha divide.

Celia proved to be stocky, generous of build, with her hair in a short permanent. She wore levis and shirt. I had already been told that she was outspoken and fearless, and that few men could excell her in handling a packstring, or in cutting out and counting sheep. She had lived in the canyon most of her life.

It was of necessity a plain lunch, without fresh meat or poultry, but Anna said the rolls were good and Celia praised my cake, with the topping baked right on it. Our two men especially enjoyed the lively conversation provided by the two ladies.

It was later, when we were sitting in the yard hoping for relief from the heat, that Anna said to me, "You speak of canning so much fruit. You don't intend to really make your home here, do you?"

"Yes I do," I said.

"But how can you with the children? I never dreamed you expected to *live* here."

"Len and I don't figure on a two-home existence. That's not our idea of the way to bring up a family."

While Anna and I talked Celia had been walking about restlessly. Now she said: "As I rode in, I saw a mare in your corral. Bay, black mane and long black tail. Could I have a closer look at her?"

"You must mean Babe," I said.

"Where did you get her?"

"Len bought her for me, two years ago. Out near Enterprise."

"How old is she?"

"We think she's seven or eight."

Dick went to bring Babe, and as the mare approached, Celia's face lighted. She put her fingers on the brand on Babe's shining hide.

"That's my personal brand! I used it some even after I married Jack. We raised this mare and we hated like everything to let her go. Did you know she's out of an Indian cayuse by a government stallion, and she has quarter-horse blood? But she's nearer ten years old than eight."

Celia fondled Babe, and tapped her neat hoof proudly. "She takes the smallest shoe you can get, doesn't she!"

Celia could hardly stop talking about Babe, and I knew why. Sheep-ranch horses are rarely beautiful, since they are chosen for utility. If a horse can be ridden and packed, and if in a pinch he can be worked on a plow, he is more valuable. The favorite horse for trails is short-coupled, stout and steady. A fast horse that had to accept the pace of a packstring would fret himself into a lather.

As to Babe, an alien now, and barren besides, I often thought what a pity if all this beauty and spirit were to perish some winter in the canyon, leaving nothing but a shining memory. I had not ridden her in a year, and could not hope now to ride her much; moreover she was too high strung for the children. To me she was the embodiment of something precious and tender, and with the falling of our fortunes, she had been one thing I was determined not to lose.

"We had to let her colt go too," Celia was saying.

"She had a colt! We supposed she'd never had one."

"That's right." Celia was running an anxious hand over Babe's knees. "Not getting stiff here, is she?"

I admitted she might be, explaining how rarely I rode.

"If you ever think of selling her—"

But I shook my head.

It was about the first of August when Len phoned that he would be in soon, and that on the fifth he would take us out for a week's vacation. By the night of the fourth, I had everything washed and scrubbed, and bread baked to leave for the men. Nothing in the garden had to be canned right then, and the apricots, more than three hundred quarts of dessert fruit and jam, were in the jars. This was our most important fruit crop, and one we shared with many of our neighbors.

Len came in afoot, walking the seven miles from Circle-C ranch. He was weary of the cries of lambs, weary of strayed pack animals and camp housekeeping. "Let's take one easy day before we start," he said. "One day of peace."

With difficulty the children and I came down from our high pitch of excitement, but two mornings later we rose knowing The Day had come. While the men got the mules and horses ready, I cleared up breakfast and the children got into their clean outfits. Then we snapped the bags shut and took them out for cargoing.

To Patsy and me Len had assigned Kate. She was a small roan mule that kept her absurdly long tongue forever out and her tail rotating, the stoutest, gentlest, pluckiest creature of our whole ranching life. This morning she wore an old saddle that I had used for years.

Len's mount was Eagle, a hard-mouthed, white-nosed bay, that could be harnessed, packed or ridden, and who would always arrive where he was going without mishap. Joe was to ride behind Len's saddle, and Steve in front, with a cushion under him to soften the saddlehorn.

Dick started ahead, leading the packmule. He would go only to Circle-C, where his coupe had been left for our use; then he would bring the horses back to the ranch.

After we rode through the gate of the lower field, the going was new for the children and me. The trail climbed by switchbacks to a shelf high above the river, narrow and full of rock stringers bare of soil. I tried to talk cheerfully to Patsy and to keep looking at some rock or bush that was level with my eyes. I told myself that horses were no more eager to lose their footing and go bounding out into the air than their riders were, and Kate's little shoes clashed steadily against the rock, with neither hesitation nor any sign of uneasiness. Finally the trail leveled if it did not widen, and I breathed easier again. Now Kate quickened her gait, her tongue still dangling, as she kept her eye on Eagle, ahead, who merely tolerated her.

Suddenly a brilliant prospect opened before us, through the shimmering heat. We could see Circle-C, where the canyon spread to permit big hay fields, and on the other side of the Snake, hazy in brown distance, lay the Titus ranch. The trail led on, in and out of vertical gullies, and I tried to trace it as it descended, climbed again, and finally swept around a high, bald promontory where the view ahead and straight down would probably take the breath.

We had now reached the farther edge of Royal Gorge, on a trail that was nothing but a thin lip. Ahead my husband was balancing the baby calmly, prodding Eagle whenever he sought to snatch a mouthful of grass from a cranny in the wall. Joe clung firmly to the saddle straps, his short legs sticking out. All was well, and I was happy to leave the pinched ledge and start along a sandy terrace strewn with cactus and rocks, though this broke off a few feet farther out. Behind me Patsy chattered.

Suddenly things were sinking under us! Kate's legs were giving way—she seemed to be stricken! Then everything went out of control and Patsy and I spilled off. We must have screamed as we hit and skidded on through the cactus, for I heard Len yell at Dick.

When I could look around, Kate was standing in her tracks, but on the ground lay our saddle, its cinch frayed in two. Patsy and I picked ourselves up, and though we were stitched with cactus and scratches, we seemed to have broken no bones. I took Steve while the men repaired the cinch with straps removed from elsewhere. Then we all remounted and the train proceeded. No one had said much, and it was the following day before it occurred to me that only a few feet of trail had separated Patsy and me from eternity.

At Circle-C I met the manager's wife. This ranch was one unit of many owned by the Campbell brothers, cattlemen of New Meadows. Mrs. Richardson was quiet and friendly, a superior woman who was used to feeding big haying and beef-ride crews, as well as a steady flow of hunters, prospectors, men looking ostensibly for work, and those other obscure people who show up at the end of any road where wilderness and escape of some kind occur together.

It was a heady feeling again to ride in an automobile, even at five miles an hour, over high-centers and around hairpin turns. The coupe crawled to the top of the ridge, then circled down through cool timber to the ferryboat on the Salmon.

In the small car we had one child on the seat between Len and me, one in my arms, one standing against my knees.

Whenever the wheels met a rock, the standing child bumped against the others to avoid the windshield, but no one complained.

In Grangeville we ordered lunch in a cafe, a gay business for me after five months of my own cooking. Steve tilted his poached egg onto the floor while I was wiping another child's face, but the waitress had an understanding heart.

Soon we were on the highway again, with new country to see, and a week of leisure ahead. In Enterprise, Grandma and Grandpa Jordan would be expecting us. Their shady yard was fun; there would be children for Patsy and Joe to frolic with. For myself a barbershop haircut, and if possible, a movie. I did not consider new clothes, for on the ranch levis were best most of the time.

I took Steve to the doctor who had delivered him, just a year before.

"He seems okay," Dr. Gregory said, at length. "Perhaps he's a little thin, but that could be on account of his teeth. You have it hot there in the canyon, I suppose?"

"Around 112 in the kitchen when you're canning fruit," I admitted.

"You've lost some weight yourself."

"About fifteen pounds," I said with pleasure.

Our contact with the greater world had shown us one thing: others were having troubles we knew little of. It was true we worked longer hours, had no luxuries, spent nothing on pleasure, and saw none of the people most dear to us. But we were confronted with none of the personal and economic tragedy that 1933 continued to produce. We had little upkeep and depreciation, no social worries, and we could think of no one in the canyon who would remotely consider blowing out his brains.

After a week that was like a day, and even with a teething baby, we were glad to start home.

We returned by the same route we had taken out, and on reaching home the children were agog to discover that during our absence the two big tabbycats left with us by a miner had each produced a beautiful family.

Fall was arriving, even in August, and it was time to dwell on new projects. One especially vital to me was the plan to move the kitchen to the basement. Such lumber as was necessary had already been salvaged from old buildings on the outfit, and we had the tools that ranches accumulate through the years, plus those we had brought ourselves. Ranches buy their nails by the keg, so there were plenty of these, and little further outlay for materials would be required. Len made all sorts of measurements and drew careful sketches, and at the first spare moment he began work.

The concrete basement walls would not be altered. There was a wide window on both east and west, each fitted with bars, to be left as they stood. First Len took down the storm door and cut it to fit the entrance to Jake Gaus's cellar. In the standard door he sawed a large square and bolted over it a four-paned window for extra light. The basement floor was rough and broken, but since mixing concrete is a simple trick to a canyon man, he just poured a new floor over the old one.

Then he attacked the kitchen flooring with bit and saw, lifting out a rectangle to make room for a stairway. Coming down, the stairs would barely miss the east window in the basement, make a right turn and stop exactly at the cellar door. Under the stairs Len built a supply cupboard topped with a drainboard sloping into an actual sink—one we had providentially brought.

From the Foust cabin he packed down a good dish cupboard, to fit into the angle of the stairs.

The top drawer of our Hoover cabinet had to be sacrificed to the sink, which came flush against it, as compact as in any modern kitchen, but that was the only loss. To the left of the cabinet there was just room for the faithful Monarch range, with reservoir intact; and when it was in place and the dining table enlarged, we saw what our new kitchen would look like. The last job was to construct a railing for the stairwell, complete with a little pole gate and bar at the top, this for Steve's protection.

With carriage red I painted the chairs and table, and for the depressing walls I found a good if unorthodox solution. Below Carter Mansion there lay exposed a high cream-coloured bank of talc, so soft it could be dug with a spoon and put through a flour sifter. I had used it for scouring camp kettles and had added it to homemade soap to make "mechanic's" soap. So now I boiled a bucket of thin flour paste, stirred in all the talc it would carry, and applied this kalsomine to the concrete walls. It hid discolorations and dried quickly. So I tried it also on the stained joists and ceiling boards. Within hours my kitchen was transformed. It was light, it smelled fresh, it looked clean. And the "paint" had cost nothing.

Later when I had put up ruffled curtains and an India block print for a hanging at the stairway, a new pad and denim cover on the chest, and new brown paint on the cupboards, we felt enormously pleased. True the ceiling was so low that very tall visitors had to take off their hats, but that meant less space to heat when winter invaded the canyon. The range would warm the kitchen; and the terra cotta flue would temper the main room above, but stove wood was always precious. We were determined to preserve the few alders that remained along the creek, and so our wood had to be brought down from the hills, loaded in rope slings on the mules, whenever they were coming home "empty."

In the new living room upstairs I painted the plasterboard a light gray and mounted a world map along the stairway. To have our pictures on the walls and our braided rugs on the floor, with a cot for a sofa and our books in cases—all this made a big difference. The bookcases had come easy: I found a half dozen wooden lard boxes of identical size, sectioned them on each other, and applied red paint. The result was a sturdy and attractive bookcase.

Through the summer when the *Chief Joseph* could not reach us because the river was too low, our mail was sent around to Whitebird, and we got it from there when we could. A rancher along the route to Circle-C might bring it to his place, and another take it a bit farther. Sometimes our magazines were well thumbed, yet few were lost, and the sacred mail-order catalogues always came through.

Having no radio we were without regular news, but down the phone line someone was good enough to set aside an evening half hour when he would remove the receiver from his phone and turn on the radio newscast. This was a great blessing, and if it irked other subscribers that summer, we heard no complaints.

For music, we had our phonograph, and in the bunkhouse there was always a sheepherder's portable with dusty Uncle Josh and hillbilly records that the children adored. I had a banjo, strung for uke chords, and we sang a good deal. The only number in which Len ever joined was "The Road to Mandalay," hardest of all to chord properly, but definitely our favorite.

In September Len contracted the lambs, then trailed

them from mountain range to the nearest railroad stockyards. The aged ewes were disposed of and those to be kept were started toward home range. Our lambs had brought four and a quarter cents a pound, a top price, but firm bargaining was not the sole reason.

Behind bargaining is good herding; and essential to good herding is meticulous camp-tending on the part of the boss. A herder who always runs out of bacon or butter, and who is left to wrestle with his problems alone, does not bring out the biggest lambs. To know what a herder should accomplish, his boss must frequently sleep and eat in camp, and must know at first-hand the range, the water and the predators likely to be met. Fortunately Len had herded sheep himself.

On our summer range the worst killers had been bear, though coyotes never scorned a lamb. On the Kirkwood range, it was coyotes and bobcats that gave us our worries. In Len's careful notes, the exact count on sheep and lambs was always recorded, and if one was missing his book showed the cause. Without records it is hard to fix responsibility.

Fall was advancing fast, and the herders were happy to be back on home range and thinking about their layoffs. As the snows fell, their camps would descend toward the warm river face, closer to the ranch, closer even to lambing and shearing, those annual headaches now mercifully forgotten.

Frost had blackened the tomato vines, and the walnuts fell amid rustling leaves. With pickling and preserving past, deer season came, and it was time to make mincemeat and can venison.

Max, a curly-haired town boy, crazy about life in the open, had come to do trapping on our range. He rode in one morning with a buck deer, its head gone and its carcass bumping stiffly.

"Where do you want it?" he asked cheerfully. "You'll have to do something with it right away!"

"Bring it in here," I said, pointing to the kitchen table.

So I put everything else aside and fell to work. Even the children could help some, and while I hacked out solid chunks of meat the right size to squeeze into a wide-mouth jar, and separated the springy muscles of shoulder and shank for separate boiling, Patsy worked on ribs. So that she should not become tired, she was allowed to labor only long enough to learn to use a small knife, and to observe that good meat is dearly won.

The hollow bones I took to the chopping block, and shattered them with an axe. It took a big kettle to hold them when they were rinsed off. Hours of boiling would bring a pot of rich gelatin broth, and with this I would fill up the meat jars.

I held out the lovely tenderloin, which lies against the backbone, tied in place with tough threads which, according to Max, the Indians used in their sewing. When it is stripped out, the tenderloin slices like butter, and I kept some of the round steak and the liver and heart for frying. Then we put aside a box of scraps for the dogs, and washed our knives and cutting boards. Our buck was no more, and we had earned a rest. I put the two-quart jars in the cellar; tomorrow they would be capped, then boiled for three hours.

It was the first deer I had ever attacked and reduced to terms without Len's help, and I felt victorious. Moreover the children had had a chance to watch the disjointing of what nature had put together so efficiently, the engineering that geared this intricate structure and enabled a deer to take a steep canyon slope at flashing speed.

The next evening as I set away the processed jars, I remembered asking a more experienced friend: "How can you be sure that your home-canned meat is safe when you open it?"

Her answer had comforted me: "If it isn't safe, you can't stand it in the house!" I longed for a pressure cooker, which Dick thought unnecessary, but even after I had it I went through some agonies of doubt. Opening a jar I would still check mechanically: "Contents must look right, smell right, *feel* right to your fingers."

Among men in the canyon, especially bachelors, it is a favorite morbid topic, how somebody's cousin died of home-canned meat or vegetables. You ask, "Now you're sure a pressure cooker was used, not just a hot-water bath?" Invariably the bachelor asserts, "Oh sure!" But suddenly his eyes flick—he doesn't know the difference!

Our herders were ever tactful about my food and canning, and eager for excuses to come to the ranch over night, though there were few of these opportunities. Now Sam appeared one evening. Len had agreed to stay with Sam's sheep while the herder brought home the packstring and secured from the bunkhouse a legal paper he needed.

Sam was blond, clean, polite, of indefinite age, and had weaknesses, as anyone would know from his deeply cleft chin. Two weaknesses likely to show up when he went for a layoff were, naturally, women and whiskey. On a layoff before we acquired Sam, he had become deeply involved with both his failings, only to find that in some hazy moment he had contracted matrimony. Anyhow the girl said he had, and he was glad to believe her. However, on the last day of his delirious leave, he gave her all the money he had left, and returned to the only job he knew, herding. Being in love, or thinking he was, had been idyllic, but the girl would need money and he had promised to be back with the sheep on a certain day.

Several months passed, during which Sam herded steadily and his wages went to the girl. Then he learned she had not bothered to divorce an earlier husband. It was a dreadful shock—at first. Then with surprising speed and no bitterness, Sam recovered—and began saving for his next layoff.

When he came to the house for supper now, I saw that he had just been washing his hair, which smelled sweet even from across the room. After supper he wiped the dishes, spoke admiringly of the food, and mentioned that his hair was very long.

"So it is," I said, going for the hair tools and the shoulder cloth.

As I clipped, he reviewed his current loves—he was corresponding with several—and asked my opinion about each. When the haircut was done and Sam had inspected the results in a hand glass, he said, "I'm sure obliged for everything; but say, would you do one more thing for me?"

"Like what?"

He grinned. "I can't understand it, but I got in from my last layoff with some bills. Will you keep them?"

There were angles to keeping a man's money that he did not perceive. "Look," I said, "I know a good hiding place. In the cellar." I took the lamp and showed him where a rock in the concrete wall was loose. It could be lifted out, disclosing a dry cavity big enough to hold a sheaf of bills. "Now you can get your money without asking me," I explained, "and nobody will ever know where you keep it."

Over the lamp Sam grinned like a gay child.

On the first appearance of the *Chief* in the fall, five months since its last run, some miners on the river below us decided to quit and get out. They had two dozen hens representing at least six breeds and many crosses. I bought them because they were at hand, and we were now in the poultry business.

On a raw evening in November, a week after the first boat, I was preparing supper. The tubular flame in the Rochester lamp hissed gently, and the stove hummed to the vibration of simmering kettles. In the soft light and warmth, the children worked at their coloring books. Upstairs the phone gave forth an uncertain tinkle. Now if too many receivers came down, and the ring was really for me, the connection would soon grow too weak to hear. So I hurried upstairs.

When I said Hello, I found Celia Titus on the line. She said, "Grangeville's trying to get you. I'll see if I can put you through. I guess you won't care if I stay on, just to make sure!"

"Stay right on," I said amused, though I was puzzled by the call.

"Western Union," a woman's voice announced. "Mrs. Jordan? I am sorry, but I have bad news for you. Are you alone?"

Alone? Why should a stranger be interested in whether I was alone. It was the first message I had had from Ada Cyr, the big-hearted, big-bosomed telegraph operator in Grangeville who had once lived on a lonely ranch herself.

"This is about a death," the gentle voice went on, "and if you are all alone I hate to give it to you."

"I can take it," I said.

"You won't faint?"

"Oh no!"

"It's a wire that says your father died this morning."

Even with the warning she had given me, I had to brace myself. She read me the details finishing with, "The funeral will be on Wednesday."

"Thank you," I said putting back the receiver. Then I sat down in the darkness trying to steady my mind. Downstairs the children were suddenly silent. I could hear the warm murmur of the stove and see the ring of light where the chimney tile came up through the floor, but my heart cried for something to fasten to, some symbol. Outside it was raining, and inside there was supper to be cooked.

Downstairs someone came in the door and hailed the children. The phone rang again. Celia spoke: "Listen. I'll keep the children for you if you want to go."

I thanked her and said I'd let her know, but this was pointless for I had already made up my mind. If I went out, somebody would have to take me to the bus, a day's ride across the divide. The children would have to be taken horseback to Celia's, which would require two men at least another day. And at Pittsburg ranch, no matter how kind and understanding Celia was, Patsy would weep herself asleep for me at night. She would not eat. By day she would stand at Celia's window, watching.

My husband came up to ask why supper was not going ahead as usual. When I told him the news, he put his arms around me in the dark. After a little while he said, "Don't grieve too hard, my girl. It's for the best. Do you want to go?"

He put the question with complete trust that I would realize it was impracticable for me to go. He left me then, and went down to tell the children as gently as possible, and Dick, who had come in.

When I had supper on the table and the several men were seated, I sat and ate a little. Dick said, "Mrs. Jordan has just got bad news. Her father died. We're all sorry, but I could of told her she would get some bad news. D'ye remember at breakfast three days ago when she said she'd dreamed of white horses and black horses, all running together?"

# 4

ON THE NEXT TO LAST BOAT BEFORE CHRISTMAS, OUR few gifts had been sent out, gifts limited to parcels of English walnuts for our relatives and friends. In the case of the grandparents, there were additional presents made by the children, with minor adult help. Our determined frugality did not ease much, even at Christmas.

In the youngsters' stockings there would be something practical and something they had longed for, with a treat of candy and oranges. However, they would be amply showered by grandparents, aunts, cousins and friends; the boat had already left numerous mysterious packages.

For the herders I was preparing a holiday box apiece, to include a dinner that would resemble their own cooking as little as possible, and such small items as pencils, writing paper, a handkerchief and a carton of cigarettes.

Suddenly word came by phone that there would be no last boat. The river had begun to run ice; it was too risky.

The things we had ordered for the Christmas stockings were due on the last boat. What would Patsy and Joe think when they skipped out of their beds on the great morning and found that Santa had failed them?

That night after the "Lay Me's" and a round of blessings on many heads, including the white-whiskered gentleman, I said carefully: "You know, Santa Claus is growing old, and they say he once got confused and was a week late starting from the North Pole."

With gravity Patsy and Joe considered this unhappy possibility.

"But he always gets here *sometime,"* Patsy said, "doesn't he, Mother?" On our trip last summer, one of her little friends had raised some doubts about Santa.

"I've never known him to fail," I said firmly.

"How's he going to make his sleigh stay on the trail?" Joe asked.

"Oh, I suppose he can leave the sleigh, and pack things on his reindeer when he has to."

"Dancer and Prancer," Joe exclaimed, jumping up to dance in his sleepers.

"And Cupid and Vixen!" Patsy cried, her eyes crinkling.

They urged me to get the poem—they had forgotten the other reindeer's names—and I had to read it all the way through before they would go to sleep.

Then four or five days later Celia phoned that regardless of ice, the *Chief Joseph* had reached Pittsburg and would be up in the morning. So our order would arrive in time, after all, and Santa's ageing inefficiency could be forgotten. In the Christmas dawn the stockings would hang plump and thrilling.

Dick went out on the boat, to spend the holidays amid brighter lights than ours. Max crossed the river and rode for hours to catch a stage to his parents' home. Our one guest at Christmas dinner would be Charles Adelbert Russell.

Mr. Russell occupied a tiny bar a mile below us, with precipitous cliffs between. He "squatted" and mined. Past sixty, spare and spinsterish, he was probably the handiest and cleanest bachelor in the canyon. He had so many tales to tell about his own cleverness, bravery and rich experience in various lines of endeavor, but particularly telephone "engineering" and the production of band music, that we never could decide why he had left orderly Michigan and come to live in the canyon. I was sure, of course, that some woman must have been responsible.

On the day before Christmas, early in the morning, Len loaded his mules with the gift boxes and the regular supplies for the herders. The children and I put in a busy cheerful day and finished by decorating the little Christmas tree with the glittering balls, the foil icicles and the tinsel garlands that had become very precious with the years. Under the tree we placed the packages that had come by mail. Outside, night had fallen down gray and fretful, but when I had milked the cow and shut up the chickens, the children and I drew together cosily in the warm kitchen. At bedtime Len had not returned, but I knew it was too much to expect. There was no trouble getting the children to bed, and when they were deep in their excited dreams, I filled the stockings.

At six o'clock on Christmas morning I waked from a dream that Len was beside me, but it was only a dream. Christmas day alone, I thought, last Christmas he was away too.

When I looked out, the air had a watery, despondent feel, but the children were unaware of it as they bounced joyfully out of bed to seize their stockings. These were so satisfying that with a little persuasion the kids agreed to leave the tree presents until Daddy came.

Things seemed better when Mr. Russell arrived, wearing a necktie, and a Christmas shirt from his sister. And just after noon, Fannie tore up the creek barking madly; then around the bend came Len, his mules creaking with slings of wood. The day was going to be perfect!

As he put on his best clothes Len explained that he would have come sooner but he'd been obliged to move Frank's camp through a fog, a wretched business when the Norths are slick. For on one point Len was adamant: he allowed no herder to go where he was unwilling to go himself. So he insisted on taking plenty of time, going a roundabout way and out-foxing danger.

The table was soon set with our best cloth and napkins, and on the rarely used table mirror was a little centerpiece of fir and tinsel with red candles. We had chicken, dressing, jello salad and mincepie—just like the herders. The children could hardly wait through dinner to get to the Christmas tree and see how Daddy was going to exclaim with wonder and unbelief over the socks and shaving lotion they were giving him.

There were small gifts for Mr. Russell too. He stayed on through the afternoon and we played diligently with the children's mechanical toys, accomplishing a great deal. At twilight Mr. Russell took prudent leave, and Len went outside to do the chores. Purely as a concession to me in my holiday black satin, he fed the chickens and latched them in, for he believed hens to be stupid and unreasonable birds, unworthy of adult male attention except when hot on a platter.

So for the lamplit evening, the Jordans were snug at Kirkwood, all of us together.

# 5

THE MILD JANUARY AFTERNOON WAS CLOSING. THE kitchen was swept, the living room tidy, and the bedrooms in order. On the floor in the kitchen Steve played with his new blocks. At a year and a half he was healthy; he talked if he chose to; and he was charming when he laughed in his own very special way, as if he knew something utterly droll.

At the table Patsy worked in her new Christmas paint book, where a water-dampened brush brought out the most bewitching colors, right on the paper. She was almost seven, and the gold bob that cupped against her peach-round cheek was as determined as her chubby hand on the brush. She labored with great intentness.

I went to feed the chickens and search for the two or three eggs they had started to produce now that the new year had begun. I had to hurry or the magpies would beat me to the eggs.

Except for Max, who had returned from the holidays

with a stubborn flu-hangover, the children and I were alone. Max was staying close by, tending only his traps along the nearest bars, which he could reach without much effort. Joe too had been in bed with a cold and was still taking codliver oil.

For an hour I had not seen Joe; he was probably in the bunkhouse with Max, playing old phonograph records. The bunkhouse was dim, with a barbequed smell, but its heater and ample bed surfaces for lounging made it a snug retreat. Still I felt a bit uneasy and I called outside for Joe. I got no answer, and when I knocked at the bunkhouse there was no reply even from Max. The children never went far from the house without telling me, and never out of whistle-call unless specially sent. I told myself Joe must be somewhere close with Max. But where? Max was taking it easy and wouldn't go far. But Joe wasn't well enough to go anywhere off the bar, and Max should not take him without asking me. Resolutely I went to the house for my coat.

"Patsy," I said to the toiling artist, "I can't find Joe. I'm going to the upper end of the bar, but if I don't see him there I'll come right back. You stay in the house with Steve."

She looked up anxiously. "Oh, Mother, don't go. I know Joe'll be right back. If you're going somewhere, take me with you!"

I explained that she would have to stay with Steve, and before she could plead further I went out. Patsy did not mind a dark room, nor doing an errand outside in the dusk, but she could not bear to be alone for a long time without me. Depressed by the look I had seen on her face, I hurried on my way. Passing through the orchard I went on by the abandoned stackyard and the "prospector monuments" at the base of the bluff. It was at least a quarter mile to the upper end of the field, where a lone jackpine stood, and where the trail had to climb around a towering headland of rock separating Kirkwood from Halfmoon.

In the sand I kept seeing two distinct sets of tracks, that of a man and that of a child. The smaller ones always lay upon the bigger ones, but this did not prove that Joe was with Max. It might mean he was an hour behind him. Striding along intently and bent on his own affairs, Max might not even realize that a four-year-old was trying to catch up with him. And it would soon be winter night along the river.

As I started up among the stone shoulders, I knew I would not be turning back until I found Joe. Below boiled the Snake, bottle green in the uneasy light. Tonight it seemed as personal as the devil himself. I wondered with sudden panic if it boiled with a new secret, a very new secret.

Aloud I said, "I'm not going to think about this until I have to. When I reach the highest turn, then I can see down the other side. I'll see Max. Joe will be with him. I'll see them from that point."

The light was flaking out of the sky, and across the river the western wall had turned a dusty purple. I could barely distinguish the white scratch of trail over there, but no one would be traveling it anyhow, no one who had seen anything. Then I asked myself, What if I don't see either of them when I get to the top?

At last I looked down onto the patch of sand and willows in Halfmoon, where an outcrop of rock made a good place for a trap-set. Nothing, nothing human was in sight. And no one was visible on the descending trail, either.

I spoke aloud, for the comfort of my own voice: "They

*could* be back in one of the bends, but oh God, why *don't* they come out?"

I waited and waited, growing colder and more desperate each moment. Then finally far down on the shadowy bar something moved. It stood up and walked. It was Max, Max by himself!

Because I couldn't breathe and couldn't think, I leaned against the rock. Then from behind Max a bobbing red thing, a little red-coated figure, ran out of the willows. I yelled, but of course my voice was lost in the immense gulf. So I sat down and drew a long breath to stop my pounding heart. After a time Max started for the trail, Joe at his heels. Now he vanished to reappear higher, swinging in a loose-jointed trot with Joe running to keep up. I yelled again, but they did not pause. In and out, ever higher, but when at last he discovered me, Max showed only mild surprise.

"Oh," he said, "what are *you* doing way up here?"

Joe was too breathless to talk. He only said, as if that explained everything, "I'm with Max."

"Go ahead," I told them, falling in behind.

Joe trotted between us, his short legs straining. I wanted to take his hand, but the trail was too narrow. Moreover, the idea would have affronted him. When we finally reached the field it was quite dark, and as we neared the house, going slow because Joe was exhausted, I could see that a lamp burned in the kitchen. Unhappily I remembered my promise to Patsy to return quickly.

The lighted lamp was significant, for she was not to use matches except in an emergency. On the step, I paused to look through the glass of the door, and this was what I saw:

The table that would seat twelve was set with plate and silver for one. Close by was the highchair, with Steve in it, bibbed and clean. On his tray were a glass of milk and a piece of bread. Patsy was coming from the cellar carrying something for herself.

I could tell that she had been crying, but there were no tears now, and her step was firm. When I opened the door she stared like one who sees a ghost.

"Patsy," I said quietly.

She still stared as Joe followed me in. Then she spoke: "I thought you had all fallen into the river. I thought Steve and I were left all alone. And Daddy would come back some time, I thought, and maybe the cow would live till he got here, but the chickens would just have to die."

How much terror a seven-year-old can take without injury I do not know. At this moment I saw that a chubby little girl had faced panic, had decided what must be done, and was doing it. It would be silly to run outside and scream—there would be no one to hear. She must give Steve something to eat and get something for herself. Then she must put him to bed and go to sleep herself.

In time Daddy would come.

# 6

I WAS GETTING LUNCH WHEN MRS. FRED MCGAFFEE and her grandson George rode in. The Fred McGaffees were our nearest neighbors up the river on the Idaho side, four hours' ride away, and Mrs. McGaffee had visited us only once before, having stopped briefly during my first weeks in the canyon. Her years on the river had put gray in her hair and compassion into her face, as well as making a competent horsewoman of her. George, at four, rode well too. He was darkly handsome and absolutely silent, as watchful as a little wild animal. Riding a big, heavy-footed horse the whole distance from Sheep Creek, holding the reins himself, he had not minded Suicide, where a state veterinarian had once been seen to get off and crawl in preference to staying with his mount.

Fred and Billy McGaffee, brothers, ran cattle together on the range that adjoined ours on the south. Flashing, dark men of superb physique, they had grown up in the independence of untamed middle Idaho, and they loved it. Both of them had married school teachers. Fred had been at Sheep Creek sixteen years, Billy and his wife Mabel at Squaw Creek for a shorter period. I had heard often about the house Fred and Gene McGaffee had built, and I knew its reputation for hospitality. So when Gene stood in my basement kitchen and said, "You have done things here that I must try to remember," a wave of happiness flooded me.

During the winter I had found enough scrap lumber to build a double-deck bunk in our room for the two boys, so as to give Patsy the west room, and she was always willing to move to the living-room cot if company came. Thus I had a place for my guests.

As we stood in the bedroom, which now had a box-and-curtain dressing table and a shelf-and-curtain wardrobe, Gene commented, "I don't know where you keep all your things."

Somewhat embarrassed I said, "They're in boxes under the bed. You couldn't possibly sweep under it."

She smiled. "Everybody does that. You can get these roll-under chests too—they're quite good."

At lunch there was a crowd of men, and we were rushed, but Gene liked it, and in five minutes she was a stranger to no one. It was easy to see why they were always deep in guests at Sheep Creek, though it was decidedly more remote than Kirkwood. After lunch while Gene helped with the dishes, my children and George, regarding one another warily, went outside. Gene and I talked about canning and preserving, and Gene said, "You should also consider methods of drying fruit and vegetables. In this climate you can *dry* anything."

I asked her about the carrots my husband had eaten at her house, where he was a dinner guest the Christmas before I arrived. Len had told me the carrots tasted as if they had just been dug. And now I wanted to know if they had been dried.

Gene said Yes and went on to describe this process and also how to cure hams of venison the way one cured pork. She described roasting venison with garlic and herbs, and I was becoming aware that there was much for me to learn about canyon cooking.

At this point Patsy slipped in, bursting to tell me all about George but seeing no opportunity to speak. George was already intensely mechanical, his grandmother had told me proudly, and just then he joined us, his overalls pockets sagging with screws.

"Patsy, where did he get these?" Gene exclaimed.

"He took them out of the washing machine that Daddy bought for Mother and had to make over," Patsy said, "but George just wanted to see if they would come out."

Gene sent the boy to put them back.

By this time I was longing with all my heart to see Gene's house, her plantings and all her snug and clever arrangements, but it seemed unlikely that I could return her visit for a long time to come.

In the morning Gene said they must leave, and their saddled horses were led over from the corral. Regardless of the nippy air, which sometimes makes horses feel mischievous, George's big beast stood like a rock while the child shinnied up its great leg, and pulled himself into the saddle with his brown, sure fingers. There he waited, silent and remote, while his grandmother said her farewells.

She took my hand. "You've never been frightened here, have you?"

"Not much," I said. "And you certainly haven't. I think you have conquered the canyon."

"Well, I've never been afraid of anything—except maybe one man."

"You afraid! Of whom?"

"Jake Gaus."

"Oh," I laughed, drawn to her by this confession of weakness, "He's all right. He just needs a *listener.*" I did not tell her of the one time I had really been afraid.

It had happened one evening only a few weeks before. At dusk I had been milking in the corral when I saw a rock start rolling from a basalt cliff, making a path through the snow, heading straight toward me. It was not a big rock, though it leaped in big arcs, and in a few seconds it was deflected and rolled harmlesly to rest.

But that it should roll at all made me aware of several undeniable facts. I was alone with three small children; there was not a horse of any kind available; the phone had gone dead that day; and though the snow was light on the bar, it would be deep in the trails above.

When Len came home I said: "If anything had happened, or some frightening person had appeared and I had had to get out with the children in a hurry, could I have made it on foot to Dick Carter's?—I know I couldn't have made it anywhere else!"

"No," he said calmly. "Steve couldn't walk that far, and you couldn't make it carrying him. But things like that *don't* happen."

So now, as she rode away, I watched Gene McGaffee, who was never afraid, and I wondered when I'd see her again. I was richer for her visit, and Patsy and Joe had made what was very rare for them, a contact with another child.

By this time my house-bound existence had begun to pall on me, and so one mild morning before the lambing rush, when Dick said he had to go to Temperance Creek and asked me to go along, I was overjoyed. He said we could have dinner with Anna and be home by four o'clock. Eagerly I consulted Len. He agreed to stay close to the house this one day, so I mounted Babe and off we went.

Up to now I had been only a mile or two up the river, and I both longed and dreaded to explore further. Dick rode ahead, and when we had cleared Halfmoon and the blunt, low ridges beyond it, he called to me that Salt Creek was opposite, on the Oregon side, and that we were now starting the climb to Suicide. At the word I began to congeal.

Suicide is a single portentous rock, the end pier of a dominant volcanic spine that runs from high in the divide to meet the Snake. As our trail ascended, without switchbacks, edging nearer the drop, it also narrowed. We made a bend and were suddenly out on the face of the cliff. Far below a segment of the Snake boiled down in a frenzied S from invisible Hominy Bar. Presently the trail became a virtual stairway, one rock step above another, each one sloping out, with a flimsy coping of small stones to mark the edge.

Dick called down, "Don't lean toward the wall that way! If you can't ride straight, lean *out!*"

Lean out! I hardly dared breathe for fear of capsizing Babe, and Dick wanted me to lean out! In anguish I prayed. If I went off this trail, who would care for my children? Why had I ever left them anyhow? Desperately I hoped that if I made it over the rock to safety there would be some other way to get home, not over this hair-raising height.

Suddenly the trail was again a trail, leading into a boulder-strewn recess. Dick said, "Get down a minute. Now you see, if your horse slips when you're leaning *in,* your weight will throw its feet over the edge."

I nodded dumbly. He moved to where he could look down on the Snake. "They say you can spit into the water from here. It's three hundred feet, I guess."

I stood on the lip of the void and timidly flung a stone, but it vanished.

"You're past the hard part," Dick said. "The down slope's easy. Did you know there are steel pins driven into the rock back there to keep the trail from breaking off?"

I said desperately, "If we have to come back this way, I'll walk this part."

"Anna rides the whole thing, and looks back and hollers at the people behind her, just to make talk!"

I thought: Anna *rides* it. And Len rides it at *night,* pulling a packstring. Even in rain and fog and snow, and even when it's a sheet of *ice.*

Kenneth rowed up a good ways in slack water before heading across. We had left the horses grazing contentedly with their reins tied up; there was plenty of grass and they would not leave. That is one difference between a horse and a man. A horse is wise enough to begin eating grass when he sees it; a man debates, wondering whether he'll find more when this is gone.

The Temperance Creek house was fascinating. Since buildings and building supplies are never discarded in the canyon, Kenneth's castle was a combination of structures, some frame, some log. One, I think, had washed in on a spring flood. The effect was rambling with numerous outside doors and unexpected little windows.

The living room had hewn beams where saddles had hung, yet a carpet covered the floor. Earlier dwellers had tried varying effects on the walls, and the frame end of the living room was a gay patchwork of wall-paper samples. Anna had cushioned rockers, small tables, lamps and bookcases, which gave the room an air of settled comfort. In her kitchen was a sink that *ran.* "Does your sink run?" is a wistful question often asked of canyon sink-owners.

Anna's dinner did not need as a foil a kitchen flashing with bright paint. It was the kind of a meal a visiting rancher goes home and describes to his wife, and it always sounds far better than anything she has put on the table in weeks.

I phoned Len to say that we had finished dinner and would soon be starting back. How wonderful it was, for a change, to be the roving member of the wedding, but I did not say so on the telephone.

One last thing I wanted to see—Anna's cellar. It was nothing less than a disused mine tunnel in the cliff across rushing Temperance. Anna and I reached it by a chain of planks with a sketchy handrail. I thought the place dank and doubtful until Anna explained that nothing ever froze there in winter and that in summer the temperature remained so low that butter would keep fresh a long time if properly stored.

"And you've never put your hand on a snake, on the back of these high shelves?" I asked Anna.

No, she never had, but I wondered if it would bother her much if she did. Anna had a reputation for coping with anything, bobcats in the henhouse, skunks under the floor, unreasonable men—anything at all.

Steve being no longer a baby, I could come closer to enjoying lambing this year, and observing more of its features.

Our household rose to fifteen souls, and now and then the population climbed even higher. The lambing rush started at the lowest place on the range, because the earliest grass was there. All lambers must have their breakfast and supper at the table, and lunches to carry. Then there were the meals that had no particular name—meals between meals.

The lamb "drop" was heavier this spring because Len had had a year to learn the range; and there were fewer "dry" ewes. Just as many lambs were born by night as by day, so Len put on a night man at once, and this person would require his meals at eccentric hours and he would carry food with him on the job. Furthermore he must be protected from clamor during the day while he slept, and it was I who must protect him.

However, my work was not all cooking and washing. Sometimes I was a dietitian for lambs as well. Every day a weak or orphaned lamb was brought to the door; sometimes it was a pair.

A lamb for whom no mother, natural or foster, can be found becomes a "bum." The chances of saving a bum are not too good, but you can't refuse the appeal of a tender-hearted herder with a weak lamb in his arms. No, we at Kirkwood were not equipped to hand-raise orphans; equipment and time are really necessary to save them.

The bum is as piteous as any human derelict. His plaintive voice and face wring your heart. Whenever he hears the screen door flap, he totters up to supplicate you, yet he refuses the bottled milk unless it tastes exactly like his mother's. And he locks his stubborn little jaws until you have to use force to get him to take the nippled catsup bottle. Then you hold him between your knees and you hate him for the way he wastes the milk and for the sour smell in the tight curls of his wool.

Presently, no matter how hard you have tried in his behalf, the bum begins to decline. His crying becomes continuous, he gets dysentery, he totters about in misery; and you are half glad if you find him dead. He is just too human. Yet the next time an apologetic herder stands at the door with an abandoned lamb, you start all over again. Of course a few bums survive and become loving pets, but they are forever alienated from the other sheep and if put into a band they refuse to follow a leader.

Late one afternoon during the first week of lambing, when I went out for a breath of air, Len called me to see a "graft." Sam was slipping the skin taken from a dead lamb onto a big twin whose mother was overburdened with two babies. Then Sam presented the changeling to the mother of the dead lamb.

She smelled it suspiciously, and stamped her foot at Sam, but the lamb instantly began bumping her bag, and her expression became as readable as print: the lamb *looked* like hers, it *smelled* like hers, and it wanted milk.

A day or two later Sam would slit off the tightening pelt, and by that time, the lamb would still smell right to its foster mother.

"I need more colored cloth to tie on the twins," Sam reminded me. "A lot of bright stuff, if you've got different kinds."

"I'll look for something," I promised, "but you've had too many twins!"

Sam followed the Basque system of identifying a ewe and her twins by identical bits of bright cotton tied to the lambs' tails and to a wisp of the ewe's wool. Len, on the other hand, preferred stamping all three animals with numbers in colored paint, and carried a tin of paint wherever he went. With a bar stamp and a semicircle stamp, any of the ten digits could be contrived. The paint did not wash or wear off, and the number served as a record.

Now I hurried back to my baking. Cookies and cake were gone; tomorrow we would be out of bread. Sandwich material was a constant problem, for if a man liked cheese in his lunch, he wanted lots of it; but if he found cheese "binding" as he delicately put it, then he must have meat, jam, or both in his bread. Some men had to have their peanut butter mixed with honey; others got hives from honey; and it was up to me to remember everybody's individual preferences.

I was learning how to *wrap* a lunch too. In newspaper, then in a cloth sack that could be knotted and hung from the belt. Some men admitted they ate their lunch as soon as they left the house, to save carrying it. But at least their right to take a lunch had been acknowledged, which was the important thing.

Our work day began at four, and often when we were abed we heard the kitchen door being opened. Late-comers were always hungry. At the very least they must have hot coffee and reheated beans. There was often a final wistful question: "You don't have any old pie layin' around, I guess?"

As the days lengthened and warmed, the drop-band moved slowly up the ridges, and the herders and lambers moved with it. At the ranch we took advantage of the calm to put in a big garden, and it was barely finished when a request came from my mother that I could not refuse. She wrote that she had decided to go to Texas for an indefinite stay, and since she might "never see me again," would I not bring the children and come at once.

It was with some trepidation that I went, for our life in the canyon would be up for trial. The visit would be both a farewell and an inspection. But to my astonishment, Mother seemed—with a few reservations—to accept our strange mode of living and whatever it was doing to the children. This fact eased the strain of the trip, but of course the unexpected expense would have to be made up in some way yet unsolved.

Returning, we required twelve hours and three buses to reach Lewiston, with only one chance to buy milk and none to get warm food. At midnight we crept into our hotel beds and were out of them at four-thirty, but now the older children knew how to dress and comb themselves, and how to take a last look around when the bags were about to be closed.

We were aboard the *Chief Joseph* for fifteen hours, shaken by the propeller, drenched by spray, eating cold food. This time there was no Grandpa to help us, and we longed only to rest our eyes on the Kirkwood skyline. Late in the day Patsy and Joe slept against the freight, and I held Steve in my arms.

Along the Snake, dusk had turned the waters murky, but the *Chief* drove on. Then Captain Brewrink came to give me the bad news. The river was too low to run by starlight, and we would have to tie up at the next landing.

"Whose place is it?" I faltered.

"Brust's. At Wolf Creek."

I had heard the Brusts mentioned—they were cattlemen—but I wondered if they would welcome complete strangers. Fervently I wished that we could just stay on board, but when we had moored the captain came with a lantern and led us over a stony ridge, through a gate and corral, and finally up a plowed field to lighted windows.

George Brust proved to be a big, easy-moving blue-eyed man with sandy hair and a drawl. He explained that his wife was teaching school this spring and was not at home. He and his men had eaten, but he opened canned peaches and brought milk for the children. There was some sourdough bread left from their supper and it tasted great.

When we had finished, Brust took us upstairs into a room that covered the whole house, with low windows all around. He showed me a bed behind curtains of clean floursacks sewed together, and pointed out a second bed for Patsy and Joe.

I blew out the oil lamp and undressed, and was getting into bed when to my dismay I heard men ascend the stairs and creak into beds in other corners. I wondered how much sleeping I was going to do!

But the next time I opened my eyes, dawn showed through the window! I dressed, lighted the lamp, and went to wake Patsy and Joe. Patsy got her bearings quickly but Joe wandered off among the other sleepers, and I heard a man's drowsy voice saying, "Go long! *I'm* not your mother! She's over there back of that curtain by the lamp."

Captain Brewrink was waiting below, and in the morning chill we made our way back to the boat. In our lunch box, we still had some graham crackers, and we munched these rather forlornly. But a surprise was in store, for as soon as Captain Brewrink could get the coal stove going, he fried eggs and made coffee. It seemed no sin to let the children sip enough of my coffee to warm their little gizzards, and they were soon as merry as grasshoppers. Behind them lay a kaleidoscopic week of new acquaintances, a grandmother, trains and buses; but ahead lay Kirkwood and their father.

When Kirkwood Rock broke into view through the heaving notch, and the tin granary at the landing grew from a dot to a structure, they could scarcely keep from screaming their happiness. But no one was there waiting to welcome us, so in a somewhat crushed mood we carried our own bags up through the empty field. The grass in the yard had grown grotesquely in a week, and everything looked forsaken. The kitchen smelled of forgotten food; in the bunkhouse no one answered our calls.

But when the children had located their hiding kittens they felt oriented again, and I addressed myself with pure pleasure to cleaning and baking, against whatever crowd the night might bring.

Soon Dick arrived, plainly relieved to have other human beings about. It was not certain when Len would be back, he said. He and the man irrigating the alfalfa at the Carter place had been batching. Actually Len came back only in time to rush off the next week's orders by boat and to confer with Kenneth Johnson on shearing plans.

We must find a shearing cook at once. Last year kind Anna had moved over to Little Bar to see us through, but this was too great a favor to accept twice; and it was out of the question for me to take three children and move to Little Bar.

Fred Ballard, who was helping through lambing, said his wife Mae might be willing to cook, and was experienced. I had seen her but once, briefly, and had found her a compact, assured woman with snappy dark eyes, no waster of words. Fortunately Mae agreed to come.

All through shearing a canyon sheepman fears rain, fears the river may suddenly drop and prevent his wool going out by boat, and fears most of all that on some strange pretext the crew will throw down their clippers and leave his sheep unshorn. Shearing sheep induces temperament, and shearers must always be treated with deep understanding. No mutton must be offered them; in fact, the word "mutton" must never be spoken. But it is permissible to put on the table veal, pork, turkey, chicken, sturgeon, fresh vegetables from the store, cream, pie if at supper, cake any time, and raw-fried potatoes constantly.

In camp a little alcohol is to be expected, but more than a little can bring on a crisis. This year one of our men had a friend who had another friend who operated a still in a ravine somewhere, and under cover of darkness this third unidentified party rode to Little Bar loaded with jugs. That he sold plenty was clear from the way a general fight began just before daylight, when the shearers should have been sleeping soundly for the day's tussle with big strong ewes that didn't want to be sheared. At breakfast the revelers straggled in, some still quarreling. Mae met them head on.

"You men can cut out the nonsense," she said in effect. "I'm not going to stand for it. Sit down and eat, then you get down to that shearing plant and make yesterday's record look silly! Do you hear me?"

Orders like that from anyone else would have blown a lid off, but Mae made it stick. After all, shearers know they can't shear sheep if there is no cook in the cook house.

Two days later, with everybody amiable, the shearing was done and the ewes were trudging back to the hills. Mae left for her home across the divide, the extra help departed, and life slowed to the torpor of June, with rattlesnakes to keep it exciting and labor in orchard, garden and field to make it profitable.

The July morning was hot and lifeless. In the blackberry thickets Len, Max and Posy, our part-time boy, were making judicious sorties on the prickly branches. I did not expect them to pick long, for men and blackberries *on the bush* are not naturally compatible. Suddenly there appeared a rider, with startling news. It was tall, lean Clay Davis from the divide, and he said that at Granite Creek Martin Hibbs lay in his own yard, possibly murdered.

Clay had a psychic sense for impending drama. He knew where fate was about to strike, and was often first on the scene, but he never managed to quite beat the event itself since distances are so great in the canyon.

And now when we had heard this startling news, I thrust aside the cookies I was baking and prepared a quick lunch. No one on the Snake ever starts anywhere without eating, and if it happens to be late in the afternoon, he eats, spends the night, eats again and *then* starts.

My husband did not ask if I wished to visit the scene of tragedy. No one suggested that if it was truly murder, the killer might still be in the canyon, waiting to strike again. Naturally all women and children were safe. Clay and my three men rode off armed and excited.

Clay had said that on the previous afternoon Mr. Hibbs' widowed daughter, who lived on the Oregon side, had crossed and ridden up to her father's place, leading pack horses and intending not only to pay him a visit but get some of the fruit that would be going to waste. But where the old house had stood there were only cold ashes now, and in the darkening yard lay her father.

She remounted and dashed back down the narrow trail for several miles, until she could shout to the Wilsons on the other side. Earlier they had put her and her horses across; now they returned for her. She was in a state bordering shock, but she managed to tell them what she had seen, and they phoned the word to the Idaho authorities in Grangeville. The sheriff and coroner had started toward Granite Creek at once, and were probably there by now. Clay, though he lived miles and hours from the affair, had garnered the whole story by phone.

Day was gone when our men reached Granite Creek, and the river had shifted from daytime green to night-time mauve. The officers of the law were in full charge, and other neighbors had arrived, but it was too late to do anything. However, there were some new findings. Not only had the Hibbs cabin been burned, but the bones of another human being lay in the ashes. Also, it seemed possible that Mr. Hibbs had been dead a week, and that he had been shot from behind as he unsaddled, for his gear was found leaning against a tree and his horse was still wearing its bridle as it grazed.

There was no place to sleep and little food aside from the fruit on the tall old trees, so the men built a fire and sat out the night around it, huddling pretty close to each other I suspect. As long as anyone could stay awake they rehashed the meager evidence, but there were no clues and no one to suspect.

Earl Hibbs had gone out of the canyon on business, which was not unusual. Two prospectors who had been working up the creek were not to be found. It was known that they had called at the ranch, but who they were, where they had gone, and what attitude they had held toward Mr. Hibbs were matters of conjecture only.

In the slow-breaking dawn, and with the officers jittery to get away from the scene, a coroner's jury was impaneled. The only verdict possible was death at the hands of an unknown person. Not knowing whose bones lay in the ruins of the cabin, the jury could do nothing of legal importance for this individual.

Martin Hibbs had lived in his canyon fastness for thirty-five years; he had been bitten four times by rattlesnakes, it was said. He had lived amid natural hazards every day of his life, yet he had died from a shot in the back while peacefully unsaddling his horse. As for knowing who had waited in the shadows for Mr. Hibbs to come, the canyon merely shrugged its shoulders over one more secret.

Only Kate would tolerate the poor corpse, but once it was in canvas and lashed on her, she marched briskly down the trail behind the other horses, no doubt with her tongue hanging out and her tail rotating. Opposite Saddle Creek the body was unloaded and rowed across the river for burial in a quiet cemetery "outside."

The Law took the quickest trail back to its car on the Salmon River highway, and the jury dispersed. My men came home that afternoon rather soberly, and Clay lingered on a little to tell me of other tragedies in the canyon.

People from outside, even practical-minded ones, sometimes spoke of an ominous air hanging over the silences of the deeper gorge between the end of the boat run and Hell's Canyon proper. But those who made their living in the canyon seldom indulged in such luxuries of the imagination, and so it was not long before the settlement of the Hibbs estate and other changes brought two of the Hibbs daughters back to live on the river with their families. They were resolute, very resourceful women. The following year Earl Hibbs brought in a bride, and built a house for her on the site of the burned cabin.

# 7

IT SEEMED A SUMMER FOR THINGS TO HAPPEN. THE Hibbs incident was still on our minds when Murrielle, the twenty-year-old daughter of the Billy McGaffees, rode down from Squaw Creek one evening on her old white horse. She introduced herself and suggested that she would like to come to Kirkwood in September as a teacher for Patsy and Joe.

At five Joe was probably amenable to learning, and at seven and a half Patsy would need numbers and writing at least to complete her basic education—she could already read. We had sought a tutor among our friends, but without luck, and we had not dreamed of finding one right here on the river.

Murrielle spent the night. By leaving time next morning, she knew a good deal about us, yet she did not withdraw her proposal. On our side we learned that she had already done a term of ranch teaching at the Wilsons' across the Snake from her home at Squaw Creek, and that she had completed the course in an Idaho normal school. She seemed sensible, dependable, sturdy, literate, humorous, understanding, and fond enough of children. Possibly with her cow-ranch background she might think sheep inferior to cattle, but of course the livestock wars and killings in the canyon were long past if not forgotten.

So now we were able to cross the teacher problem off our minds and concentrate on the canning and farm work that must be finished before the children and I could have a summer outing. Len would get no vacation except that of taking us out and picking us up later.

This time we rode up the river, straight into an afternoon sun shining so nakedly upon the walls of Halfmoon that I thought I should faint for air. I rode first, on Babe, Patsy and Joe following on Kate. Last came Len on Eagle, leading the packhorse and holding Steve on his usual cushion over the saddlehorn. Around Steve's middle was a wide strap that had been slipped through his father's belt, and he clutched confidently at the reins as if it were he who controlled the kingly Eagle.

Behind everybody came Belle, a pepper-and-salt canine that had been given to us, and whose talents as a sheepdog were still to be proved. Just now she was really too heavy to go visiting or to present a nice appearance, but she refused to remain at home.

As we filed out upon a high bare shoulder beyond the cliffs, I could see the scarves of timber five thousand feet above, but they looked wilted against the steel reflector of the sky, which threw a harsh light into the equally harsh and surly Snake. Thinking about the pitiless sky and river, I found myself upon a boulder that had rolled into the trail before I was even aware of it. It was close to three feet through, and nearly filled the trail. I was afraid that Babe could not pass between it and the edge, but to leave the trail, either above or below, was out of the question. I doubted Babe's stiff knees could get her over the rock—and here was Kate coming up behind me.

"Len, a big rock's rolled into the trail," I shouted back. "I don't think Babe can get past it!"

"Then see if she can go *over* it," Len answered calmly, "and stay on your horse!"

But I knew Babe's limitations, and the thought of her getting unmanageable or frightened decided me. I slid off and took her reins. She pulled back, then came on unwillingly. But she made it on top of the boulder and then down, awkwardly and perhaps with pain. Kate was advancing with no change in pace.

Len called: "Patsy, give Kate her head, and let her take it the way she wants to. Both of you hold on tight."

I held my breath while the little mule sized up the situation. Slowly she lifted her forefeet. The children sat motionless, grinning, their fingers clenched to straps and saddlehorn. Calmly Kate heaved her front, hoisted her stern, caught with her heels, and slowly leveled down to the trail again.

"Mother," Patsy cried, "can't we do it again!"

Having pulled the packhorse close for the necessary slack, Len kicked Eagle up to the boulder. Eagle groaned but gathered himself for the lunge while Steve laughed with delight.

I did not remount. I must seem to *prefer* walking, rather than let the children know I had been alarmed. Babe led well enough, but when the trail began the dread ascent to Suicide, I picked a wide place and mounted, earning a silent nod of approval from Len.

Today Suicide seemed less frightful, or perhaps this time I knew what to expect. At any rate we advanced up the side of the cliff without pause. Below boiled the Snake; above, the rock went up and up. The only sounds were the clink of steel shoes on rock, the creak of saddles, and the blowing and puffing of the horses. At the hot three-hundred-foot recess, I thought Len would surely call me to stop, but he was intent on the complicated business of pulling the pack-horse, holding Steve steady, and guiding Eagle with knee and spur.

In his starchy white shirt Steve looked like a little broiled shrimp on a cracker, yet when I asked him how he was doing, he said, "Just fine!" And as we descended from the last height, Patsy called, "I'm so glad we've got Suicide on our ranch!"

At Big Bar Kenneth awaited us, and the children were both careful and excited as they took their seats in the boat. Len held the ropes of the horses, coaxing them into the water as the boat pulled away. The horses felt excited too, at the cool touch of the water, and Babe was inclined to change her place and confuse the ropes. Belle started swimming, but the current caught her and took her down. A hundred yards below she battled across to a rocky bar, and when we reached Kenneth's little dock, she was already there, panting and wagging proudly.

At Anna's, due to some superior management that she exercised, the porch on the river side was cool, and there were no flies. Moreover, she had a big pitcher of cold lemonade waiting. Her lawn was green and shady, and children and puppies were allowed to roll on it.

I was glad just to sit and marvel on how safe the tawny canyon now seemed. An hour ago it had threatened me with disaster. Now it wore an air of positive amusement.

At supper Anna served us creamed chicken and biscuits in the living room, with the shades drawn against the heat. And when it was bedtime she offered Len and me her room, telling us a story about it before we retired. She said that a woman had stayed alone in this room one night and awakened to find a pair of rattlesnakes lying between her bed and her baby's crib. All possible help was across the creek at the bunkhouse and out of earshot.

The snakes either decided to crawl away, or the woman reached a gun and shot them, Anna did not remember which.

However, I had already killed my summer's rattlesnake, and perhaps for this reason no vipers investigated us that night. By six o'clock in the morning we were at breakfast, then as soon as our horses were saddled we were on our way.

The new trail would take us straight up Temperance Creek, then climb to the Imnaha-Snake divide. We would pass Memaluse Ranger Station, and reach a road upon which Grandpa would meet us with his car.

The children and I had seen these ridges only in blue and lofty distance, and we were eager to see them closer. The cool of the creek soon gave way to the simmering heat of bare hills, and by mid-morning Steve was asleep in his father's arms. But Babe offered no objection to the packhorse so I could relieve Len of that responsibility. At noon we stopped by a spring in a ravine and ate the sandwiches Anna had prepared for us, but Len said we were still a long way from the road. No one complained about heat or saddle sores, and Patsy yielded her place to Joe so that he could have his turn holding Kate's reins.

At three we passed the silent ranger station and at last were on the road, but it stretched ahead of us quite empty, and I began to feel apprehensive. Len must start back soon to reach Temperance Creek tonight, and just what would the children and I do in this silent plateau of open pine if no one came?

But suddenly we heard the sound of a motor, Grandpa's!

At the old white house in Enterprise Grandma had a birthday supper ready, with a cake for Joe and little wrapped surprises for everybody. But even as we celebrated I kept seeing Len and his horses plodding down a dark trail, headed back to Kirkwood, where there was no one now but Mr. Russell, who had agreed to do the chores.

A few hot days later, on a thundery afternoon when Len and his pick-up crew of three had finished haying and were starting for the river eddy to swim, the phone rang sharply. It was one of the Wisenor boys calling from the Oregon side.

"Do you want help with your fire?" Rufus asked.

"We haven't any fire," Len assured him.

"Oh yes you have! A big one, spreading fast, around in Halfmoon where you can't see it. Wes and I'll get there as fast as we can, but don't *wait* for us!"

Since a grass allotment is not made on the assumption that any of it will go up in smoke, a grass fire is a serious matter. It travels faster and cools quicker than a timber fire, but it burns up profits just the same.

So Len rushed to load all the spare horses with ten-gallon cans of water and bales of gunny sacks. Then he stopped to phone the nearest United States Forest Service office, four or five hours away by any mode of travel.

"You bet! We'll get help to you tomorrow morning," the office promised. It was fire-hazard season, and they were probably fighting other fires.

*"Tomorrow morning!"* Len said. "Then don't bother!"

About dusk the Wisenors joined our men on the roof-steep slopes of Halfmoon. The flames would have to be beaten out with wet sacks, or stopped with spaded furrows where that was practicable. Back-firing would work when the wind generated by the fire itself was in the right direction. Against the fierce light there was no visibility, and without warning a man could step backward over a ledge into nothingness. If his back was toward the flames he might be able to see, but he wouldn't see much.

Because the trail would stop the fire at the lower side, Len limited his efforts to confining the wings and keeping the head from racing to the top. It was a pity a fire must start here, for the Halfmoon bunchgrass was some of our best.

By daylight the fire was out, except for smoking clumps of brush. The total loss looked to be less than a thousand acres. Thankfully Len started to collect horses, tools and helpers. But two of the men, the hay hands, who were strangers in the canyon, did not come in answer to his shouts, and no one had seen them for a good while. However, they would surely discover that the fire was spent and start for the ranch.

In the kitchen Len made breakfast while Mr. Russell and the Wisenor boys did a leisurely washing up. There was no point in waiting, and the four began to eat, though Len was a bit troubled.

And then the missing men limped in, black and smoked, but full of a sense of adventure. In the glare and confusion before dawn, they had become separated from the others, and decided to work down a slope about whose contour they could tell nothing whatever. Suddenly in the murk they came to a ledge. One of them lay on his stomach and dangled over, expecting to ease himself down. But when his feet found nothing, and he could see nothing, he changed his mind. Instead they turned up the hill again where the fire was burning itself out. Still unable to see anyone else, they climbed quite to the top of the unfamiliar ridge. Dawn finally showed them that danger was over, but they had missed their way and taken a circuitous route back to the ranch.

Since no one had had any supper the night before, breakfast was two meals in one. Len is a good camp cook, and in his gratitude he must have outdone himself. The sensible, stocky Wisenors were in no hurry. They had lived in the canyon a long time, and foolish hurry didn't seem to get folks ahead much faster. So they all sat around eating more hotcakes and reviewing other fires. They went on to review the state of the nation, and when this was disposed of they congratulated themselves on putting out a potentially bad blaze without aid from "government," and called it a morning.

Len came for us by car, but he could not linger. So in eight hours' time we drove nearly four hundred roundabout miles toward Kirkwood, bypassing the Imnaha, Snake and Salmon canyons and their intervening divides. A crow could have winged it in half an hour.

Len had expected to take us directly home, but in Grangeville his plans changed abruptly. Lamb buyers were waiting, so we drove on toward our sheep, crossing the Clearwater Canyon, a commanding if lesser gorge than the Snake or Salmon, and wound up through miles of timber to our Pilot Rock camp. The two buyers followed in their car.

Within twenty minutes after reaching Sam's camp I

found myself getting supper for quite a party—two businessmen in "store" clothes, two herders, Dick Maxwell, and our family of five—with utensils and dishes for four people at the most.

Fortunately there was plenty of food. We could have lamb (a young wether), potatoes, and canned tomatoes. Sam mixed sourdough biscuits for me, since he knew his own jug best, and he had them rising while I put together a cake. The camp was out of raisins and contained no flavoring extracts, so I used chopped dried peaches for accent. There was no flour sifter or measuring cup, and the tiny oven heated first on one side and then on the other.

Sam's bread turned out light and nicely crusty, but my cake was mournful and heavy. Yet Sam sniffed it with glistening eyes, and when the buyers ate it with stewed prunes swimming in canned milk, they pronounced it very tasty.

After everyone had finished, Sam and I cleaned up the dishes while Len made beds on the ground. I was too tired from a day in a small car with three small children to listen long to the bargainers around the campfire. At intervals their voices came to me, Len's patient, Dick's aggressive, and the buyers holding their position.

Len was depressed when he turned in. A month earlier, six or even seven cents for the lambs had seemed a sound hope. As he pulled off his shoes he said, "Our lambs are good—they admit it—but four thirty-five a hundred is their top bid, and it's better than they have offered anybody else around here. The government's begun meddling with the marketing of sheep and wool the way it's meddling with everything else the country produces! So private buyers aren't going out on any risky limbs!"

The next day Len hurried the children and me to Grangeville, to the only tourist camp with a vacancy. We were to stay there while he went back and started the ewes and lambs to the railroad stockyards.

The tourist place was built along a creek, and the running water and big shade trees made up for the one-room cabin with wood stove and scarred furniture. The easy atmosphere of a camp like this was as fascinating to us as it was new.

Indian summer had come, but now forest fires in the mountains on three sides of town turned the hazy air an acrid orange. At picnic tables in the middle of camp, women in beach pajamas played cards all day long, some of them solemn, some scatter-brained. They were not so much vacationing here as they were enduring the depression. Their husbands seemed to be working somewhere, or hunting work, and the women got meals only when their men came home. Their children bridged the day with peanut-butter sandwiches, which they had to spread for themselves because their mothers were too busy exercising their social rights.

In place of cards, one young woman pieced quilts. Her little girl had already started to school, and I could not see how they managed so well in their flimsy cabin, which was no larger than ours.

Another woman, an ex-school teacher, had taken a job as a pastry cook at the hotel, which made her something of an artist. When she returned to camp late each afternoon, her silent husband put her in the hammock and waited anxiously on her demands. Their boy had also begun school. I felt sure that this family too had been washed up by the depression.

Late one night Len was knocking at the door. He was exhausted from the hard days of trailing along dusty roads, breathing dirt and smoke, eating half-cooked food on the run, and drinking from any water hole that was handy. He said, with an air of desperation, that he must start us home right away, while he could. By this time I was quite ready to go, for dysentery was running through the camp. It might not be infectious, but it made Kirkwood look very attractive.

The next morning I went to the telephone office, and after a long wait secured a connection with the Forest Service line which through fire season was kept open to the Billy McGaffee ranch. I only wished to ask Murrielle to postpone her coming to teach the children. But even though I could hear her voice, I was not permitted to talk. When the Forest Service operator found that my business was non-Forest, he said there were fires here and there and if the line was being used unofficially some fire message might fail to get through. I insisted that I could cover everything in one sentence, or would trust him to relay my message, but the answer was still No.

Early the next morning we were packed and ready to leave, although I hardly knew whether to start at all, for Steve was obviously a sick little boy. Nevertheless we got into the car and in three hours had crossed the Salmon by ferry, climbed the divide, and braked down to Circle-C, where Mr. Russell had the horses waiting. Since he never rode, he had already started back afoot.

Anxiously we set out across the hay fields to the river trail, Steve riding in front of his father. It was now nearly noon, and as we angled up into the rims, the river breeze failed and the heat struck us in blistering waves. We climbed through a volcanic notch, then down into the parched bed of China Creek, where it spread through dusty willows to the river. Steve began begging for a drink.

"Can't we find some water for him?" I urged Len.

"There's only the river. You're not going to let him drink that!" Len said harshly.

"It will take two hours to get home, and it's getting hotter all the time."

"In the condition he's in, he ought to wait," Len asserted. He was strangely savage tempered, wanting no river water himself and determined that no one else should drink any or otherwise delay us. Nevertheless I took Steve down into the shade of the willows, where I washed his hot face with river water and let him sip a little from my hand.

By two o'clock we had descended the last switchbacks, traversed the dry field, and crossed our shriveled creek. The only shade the whole way had been that of some stunted thorn trees overhanging the trail at one point.

On the porch at Kirkwood stood Murrielle, waiting calmly. She had had lunch, and we ate some of Mr. Russell's cold biscuits and found fruit and milk. The older children soon adjusted themselves to the jungle-like appearance of the overgrown yard, and the dusty rooms. The cats and kittens came out of hiding, but of the dogs, Fannie acted indifferent about our return, as was her nature, and Belle could not escape long from her puppies. Queen was gone. She had become old, cranky and miserable, and had been disposed of.

Steve drank a little milk, then lay wanly on the padded chest in the kitchen.

Mr. Russell departed, and though it was Sunday afternoon the dirty house must be brought to some sort of terms. Murrielle unpacked her things in the room she was to share with Patsy, with no critical glances at the dust on floor and windows. She also knew just how much to help me, without embarrassment on either side.

By morning I was very uneasy about Steve, who toward midnight had fallen into a jittery stupor. But Len said, "Don't expect me to stay! I can't. By the time I get back to the sheep they'll be out a hundred head—lose them in the smoke and dust—and never know it."

So, early that morning while the trail was still in shadow, Len left afoot for Circle-C, looking thoroughly wretched.

And now my principal task was to get school started. Of course Steve must have attention, and there were chores inside the house and out crying to be done, but school had priority.

We had decided to use the south room at Carter Mansion, which would need a stiff scrubbing and a general cleaning. I knew also that there would soon be sharp mornings when heat would be necessary for an hour or two. So after Len had gone I went up and cleaned the school room, and after dinner Murrielle and I hoisted an ancient stove onto a packsaddle on Kate. Neither of us knew how to pack, but we tied the heater clumsily to the saddle forks and started out, Patsy leading the mule and Murrielle and I walking alongside with a hand on the load. Joe stayed at the house with Steve.

Through the vicious nettles and cheat grass we went, back and forth across the creek, and finally around to the kitchen door of Carter Mansion. There we unloaded our prize, and in no time had it set up inside and a fire going to test the chimney. Now we adjusted the kitchen chairs to the right height, with boxes for the children's feet. Murrielle put in place the texts she had brought and I added the books I had secured from a library-approved list. School was ready to open.

Tomorrow I might get started putting up the late fruit

and vegetables, but the accumulated soiled clothes and the summer towels and blankets would have to wait until Steve was better. Now, before the quick evening faded I must milk Brownie. The children and Murrielle helped me willingly with supper, and after that we were soon abed.

The next day Anna Maxwell phoned to ask how we all were. She had been alone most of the summer, and had had a monstrous time with skunks, practically an invasion of them. But that was all past now. She was sympathetic when I told her about Steve, and said that though she hadn't tried it herself, flour browned in a skillet with hot water added was said to be soothing.

I thanked her and said I'd keep the flour in mind.

Four days after Len left, Celia phoned that Grangeville had been trying for hours to ring me—the line must be grounded somewhere. Uneasily I recalled Len's days of sleepless, dusty trailing, and his ragged temper and haggard looks when he left. Still I was not prepared for the message that came over the wire.

A woman who kept a private nursing home was on the line. She said briskly: "Mrs. Jordan? Well, your husband is here at my place and he's awfully sick. If things get worse you ought to come, but it would be best if you came now without waiting."

"What does the doctor say he has?" I managed to ask.

"Typhoid. And he should have been in bed days ago."

"I can't come now," I faltered, overwhelmed. "But won't you please try to phone me every day, how he's getting along?"

"I'll do my best," the woman said, "but this phone line's awful, isn't it, and you really ought to come."

The news from the nursing home was never good. Day after day was the same. Sometimes it seemed to me I could not stand much more of this uncertainty. Then one morning Murrielle got up looking greenish; she was plucky and stayed on her feet, defying flu. Another morning I returned to bed after breakfast, but soon discovered that it was easier to stagger about than to lie thinking of the things that cried to be done, and of poor Steve.

Patsy and Joe stayed strong and frolicsome, and gradually Steve began to mend. Now he could retain boiled milk and gruel. But I was not done with him yet, for a day later he began coughing abruptly in a rapid, strangling way, and after an hour or two of this, I got down the doctor book and was forced to admit the truth: he probably had whooping cough.

Len lying on his feverish back among strangers must be grieving that I did not come, and I decided I had better have the woman tell him this last development—assuming he could be told bad news. A gray, fine rain began the afternoon that whooping cough arrived, and when there was nothing more I could do for Steve, I put on an old coat and boots and went up the creek. Just past the tin gate I turned abruptly to the left and scrambled up a steep ridge, where I could enjoy my misery unseen.

It was a thin ridge that fell off sheerly right into the elliptical meadow with the lone poplar tree. That was on the west. On the south it dropped into the creek. Probably the ridge had once been continuous to Kirkwood Rock, which was practically leaning over me. Maybe in some long ago past a lake had backed up behind this ridge, finally piercing it to reach the Snake, at whose edge our present Kirkwood Bar had then been built up.

The rain stopped now, and I could look up to the veiled heights on the north, back of which would lie Peter's Bedstead, no doubt thoroughly soggy now. Far away and high, on the east, was a region too precipitous for ranching, but secret enough in other days for operating stills, and here was where Kirkwood Creek had its headwaters. The savage spur that terminated in Kirkwood Rock shut off the south sky. High up and out of my line of vision, this spur had sent another branch beetling down to make Suicide and leaving the grassy triangle of Halfmoon between.

I could see the Oregon wall but dimly, for its peaks were lost in cloud, and along the trail over there no life moved. Everything seemed wet and sad.

Often in cold and spiteful weather, when Len was away on the range for four or five days at a time, I would dwell at night, despite his orders, on the fact that he might be dead. His horse could have slid where a trail had rotted, or a rolling rock could have crushed him, or a gun misfired. Nevertheless I always ended on the conviction that if he lay dying, with no hope of anyone coming, and if he reached for me in desperate fear and longing, I would know.

So now, calmed in some fashion by the sorrowful waste of ridge and rock around me, I felt that if my husband needed me above all temporal things, I would be made aware. Feeling almost cheerful, I clambered down through the dripping brush and went home to wait a little longer.

In the kitchen Murrielle was piecing quilt blocks and telling the children Salmon River tales. Her composure comforted me further, and that evening the telephone brought news, though whether good or bad it was hard to say. Len's typhoid fever was on the mend, but now he was beset by a painful pleurisy; and there was a strong possibility of pneumonia following pleurisy.

The nursing-home woman delivered her message calmly, then changed the subject to Steve's whooping cough. "Give him strained flax-seed tea with lemon juice," she directed. "You can put in some sugar to make him take it."

I was lame in my thanks, for we had no lemons and no way to get any.

Steve was definitely better, and when I could look into his mouth without starting a paroxysm, I made a discovery. He had four stunning new molars! Dysentery, whooping cough, new teeth, all in a period of three weeks! For even a determined child like him, it was quite an accomplishment. Moreover, he now demanded food.

It was a day later that our big news came: Len did not have pneumonia; he was sitting up and walking around a bit; and barring a set-back, he would be able to leave for home next Monday.

All Monday I flew. After lunch the children added their excited help. We had the washings all caught up now, including the strange-smelling things from the bunkhouse. We had baked and brewed, and the house shone with order and cleanliness.

Dick Maxwell would bring Len, but it would be foolish to expect them before five o'clock, although Mr. Russell would have the horses waiting at Circle-C hours before they were needed. Murrielle had hiked down to Mr. Russell's yesterday to ask him to make the trip. Celia Titus had also phoned us that the rain had hurt the divide road very little, and we floated on clouds of anticipation.

At three, Patsy said, watching my face: "I think they are down to the river now, don't you?"

"They could be," I smiled.

"Won't the lady there call you up when she sees them coming?"

"Perhaps not. She has so many men to cook for now and she'll be very busy."

It began to get dark outside, and we had had no word.

They must be nearly to the ranch, probably taking it slowly. And then the phone rang. It was Mrs. Charlie Cone on Deer Creek, along the road they would use.

"Mrs. Jordan? Now don't worry the least bit, but the car went off the road with your husband and Mr. Maxwell. They brought your husband to our place."

I must have gasped.

"We're taking good care of him. Charlie and Sam Robinson got our horses and Sam's and pulled the car back up to the road, and it's not hurt much because a tree stopped it. Your husband says to tell you they'll make it to the ranch tomorrow some time."

I hope that I thanked Mrs. Cone—I cannot remember. Tomorrow, I was thinking. Tomorrow it will be something else! Something *worse*. He will *never* come!

At Circle-C they promised to take care of our horses for the night, and sadly the children and I resigned ourselves to waiting yet another day. Murrielle as usual cheered us up, and after supper we had some games of Old Maid and went to bed. Steve still slept with me, and I pressed gratefully against the woolly little boy. He had been harried so long; now he dreamed as peacefully as a snow rabbit. I too found blessed rest.

At noon the next day Joe came running in with the news that two men on horses were descending the switchbacks above the lower field. Now they were coming through the alfalfa. Now they were fording the creek.

At the house Len dismounted slowly. "Hi," he called with a pretense of gaiety, "I'm hungry! What you got to eat?"

He ate a good lunch, but his mind was not on his illness, or on us. He was thinking about *sheep*. However, he had brought a bag of lemons, and belatedly we all drank a round of flax-seed lemonade, finding it soothing spiritually as well as intestinally.

Empty of young romance though the canyon seemed, three brides slept in our west bedroom the spring of 1935—slept with presumed peace although the bedsprings, which had come with the ranch, were remarkably poor. But a bed in the canyon is a bed!

First came Hazel, who had just become Mrs. Kenneth Johnson. Stiff from her long ride in, she dismounted slowly, and opened our acquaintance that evening by calling me "Grace." This was typical of her candor and adaptability. She was trim, blue-eyed, and had a glint of red in her hair and a flutter of freckles. During her brief stay she proved surprisingly aware of ranch problems, and although she would have Anna to help her as soon as lambing began at Temperance Creek, she seemed eager to get into those myriad activities about which, as a town girl, she was supposed to know nothing. Breadmaking worried her, but Kenneth assured her with some cynicism that there was plenty of Yeast Foam at the ranch; and when the honeymooners were ready to depart I gave her a big loaf of bread as a tide-over.

Next Earl Hibbs stopped on his way out, stating that when he returned he would bring a bride, a girl who had just finished college, and they would spend a night with us. This gave me time to worry, for I was sure that any college girl not native to the canyon would be depressed by our table conversation, especially a graduate in Fine Arts.

But it turned out quite the contrary, and Esther Hibbs was more at her ease than the rest of us. She wore her thick black hair in a smooth bob, and her round face was interestingly dusky. Already she managed a horse with skill, and since she had previously visited at Granite Creek, she knew what to expect there. One spring she had come with an excursion party to the end of the boat run, and Earl had conducted her and her mother to his ranch.

All I could offer these newly-weds was a half-gallon of apricot butter, but Esther made sure the jar was securely packed on the horse next morning.

Our third bride was something of a surprise. When I broached to Murrielle our decision to close school at the end of February, before lambing was in swing, she said calmly that this change would fit her plans nicely. In fact, if we wished, she would teach Saturdays and close sooner so as to advance the date of her marriage to Jimmy Wilson.

The affair had all the earmarks of Western romance. Last year Murrielle had taught the young man's sisters and brothers, right in the Wilson living room, and might still be teaching them except that the Wilsons had moved to town for the winter. Jimmy was tall and brown, Murrielle a sturdy blond; fortunately both of them loved horses and canyons.

Jimmy had paid her a week-end visit at Kirkwood. Another time he came by to take her to a dance on the Salmon. He strummed my banjo and sang for us; and in the bunkhouse he held his own against practical jokers. Having grown up on his father's cattle ranch, Jimmy aimed to run cattle for himself, or get into the Forest Service. In public, the pair behaved with great decorum, and we could see no flaw in their plan except that it would take Murrielle out of teaching.

A few days after school closed, they rode through on their way to a parson. Later they returned to spend a night with us. We could only give our teacher a small gift and wish her happiness, but at least we could do this with great sincerity.

During the winter Murrielle had taught me an amusing game. You can play it with others, or even by yourself, and it beguiles you when you cannot sleep.

You select a person whom you think you understand, partially at least, and then you decide what type of architecture he most resembles—anything from a woodshed to a mausoleum. You link his obvious traits to the analogous structural details of your building, and if you have chosen the latter cleverly, a startling picture of your acquaintance emerges.

For instance there was Dave, who sometimes stopped at the ranch, a thin, prosperous, unmarried, graying man with a deferential air toward women, though Murrielle and I were sure he only awaited opportunities. He wore clothes that were expensive, he was tight with his money, and except for a slight physical defect, he would have been openly conceited. Dave, we decided, was a tall gray brick with iron-lace, masonry arches over the narrow windows, a high stoop and tall rooms inside. The rooms would have wallpaper in squiggly patterns. A dark back stairs would lead to a damp basement, a stairs with one step missing half way down.

Murrielle knew people who were cozy bungalows or pillared libraries. I knew some spinster antiquities that were shockingly modern once the front door was opened. Between us we isolated a gaily stuccoed little cottage with geranium-red casements and a one-room interior crammed, however, with frightening junk. We never tried the game on each other—so far as *I* knew.

This nonsense started me doing more thinking about people. The friends I could not see here in the canyon came to have deeper significance, even if I weighed and enjoyed them while standing at the dishpan or pulling weeds. It was amazing how many wonderful and satisfying people I had known! Then I found myself thinking in smaller circles, and pondering the effect of the canyon itself on those who came here.

The canyon could make and break a man. For example, a stockman might come in full of ambition—I could think of several who had. The canyon would let him do well, and he seemed to be on his way to success. The opportunities here were unusual, because of the favorable climate and the good range—the range remained good because it was inaccessible. The stockman could have the range as long as he paid his fees and used it right.

So, before long, he found himself on his financial feet, but he should not assume therefore that the canyon liked him and had put him in the permanent file. At this point the man tended to grow satisfied and a little lazy. One day he might become careless on the trail and roll with his packstring; or he might be rowing across the river and forget to watch, whereupon a hidden boil would catch him. Perhaps he emerged safely that time, but he shouldn't let it happen again.

Two years have passed, three or four. Our man is older now; he is full of self-esteem because of the way he has added to his land and stock. He sees that he is abler than other stockmen; he insists on their recognizing his superiority. Meanwhile there is somebody he loves and must depend upon, but distrust infects their relationship.

All of his moves become selfish, and he is determined that whenever there is a disagreement it must be settled his way. Ugly temptations steal into his daytime thoughts; he loses the clear, open look he used to have.

His neighbors cease to turn to him; he is no help and no comfort to anyone. It is better to avoid him.

Now he should have left the canyon—according to my theory—after it yielded him what his ability and his labor entitled him to. But he didn't do this, so now he suffers the penalty: he becomes ugly; he goes on to become treacherous.

The closing of school accented a problem for which we must find an answer. Our partner, Dick, disliked the school arrangement, although we bore the cost. His health was poor, it was true; and some household arrangements, including the food, did have to be shaped with this in mind.

But the actual issue was larger.

At the outset it had been agreed that Len and I would manage the ranch and assume responsibility for the end results. To ranch in the canyon methodical, long-range planning is absolutely necessary, and in addition one must provide a basis of good understanding with employees and have the physical stamina to keep going hours after it is time to quit.

If there is countermanding of orders, or reshuffling of authority, the enterprise collapses.

Unfortunately, too, a canyon is no place to nurture grievances. The walls never talk a man out of dissatisfaction. The effect is, indeed, the opposite. If a dissatisfied man whispers into an ear already eager for mischief, the walls snatch up the word and toss it back and forth in magnified implication.

At a ranch-house breakfast table men may sit together who hate each other, carrying grudges big and grudges absurdly small, grudges wrapped in reality or in hallucination. Men may ride forth in the morning filled with passions they will nurse all day long unless distracted, and then gather again at supper and pass each other the fried potatoes with no sign of enmity. With entirely good logic, men ride the canyon trails with gun strapped on. And in the fog of a winter afternoon, where the trail winds through brush in the bed of the gully, suppose a gun speaks. Who can say whether it spoke in self-defense? Or night falls along a trail high above the river where a man rides alone—it was known beforehand that he would ride there after dark, alone. Suppose his horse stumbles and goes off. Who can say why the horse stumbled?

A canyon is a bad place for real wrongs, far worse for fancied ones.

With lambing and shearing endured, we must make ready for trailing to summer range. Nevertheless, Len and I took time to look at a possible plan for the fall, a plan to assume the upper half of the ranch. It would mean our moving to Little Bar, which was quite barren, but Dick could not be expected to leave the comforts of Kirkwood Bar. His physical limitations were real. We would have to make the Little Bar cookhouse do for a dwelling until we could build something else, but at least it had a good stone cellar.

That week Forest Ranger Clover made one of his periodic visits. He was a big reflective man, and his calls were a high point even to Patsy, with whom he often drank a cup of doll coffee while inquiring about crises at the playhouse level. We felt that he valued our efforts to preserve and improve our allotted grass, and that he would be helpful and his recommendations wise if the matter of dividing the Kirkwood range was brought before him.

Clover made his routine inspection, staying over night and leaving the usual bills under the sugar bowl. The Forest Service required its men to pay, he explained. Nothing was put in their personal pockets by our refusing the money. Clover never repeated any gossip he heard on his rounds, and he could talk well on many subjects. Whenever he stayed with us we were late getting to bed.

For the children and me, that year's vacation was one long to remember. We camped at Pilot Rock, six or seven thousand feet aloft in the airy lap of the Continental Divide. Len had set up two tents, with an outdoor dining table and a rodent-proof granary for camp supplies and for our extra clothing and leather bags. We could eat inside if a thunder storm rolled down from the eastern peaks, and one such storm did come, at night, striking with such fury that our tent seemed the target of the whole barrage. We stood about shivering and jumping, watching the bolts set fires where they hit, not always far away, and wondering if our spruce grove would be next. Water sluiced through the tent, but that seemed trifling. Toward morning the rain ceased and we went back to bed. The next day the Forest lookout on the ridge above us was relieved, for the lightning had struck his tower despite deflecting wires, and he had been shocked and deafened.

Sam Baird's camp was only an hour away, and he could dash in to dinner with us nearly every day. Ben Beaudry, the other herder, also came sometimes. He was herding near a huckleberry hill, and when he brought me a sample quart of fruit, it sold me on an excursion to his camp.

We rode over early and picked all morning, filling our buckets and kettles, as pleased with Ben for suggesting the trip as we were with our harvest. We cooked dinner and sat around visiting while the children played with Ben's dogs.

Day was darkening in the little basin where the tent

stood; it was time for Ben to go on his evening rounds. The spot seemed desolate to me, but evidently it suited the herder. He said the only time he was ever lonely was when he was camped on some bald point right up over the Snake where he could see riders far below on the trail but would never be able to hail them. If he *saw* no one he was all right.

Tired and contented, we started home. Then Len's ever-listening ear caught a suspicious sound—it might mean a strayed ewe, and if she were alone, some beast would get her before morning. "You go on with the packhorse and the kids," Len said, handing me Nig's lead rope.

We had made a half mile or so when the big mule sawed back sharply on my arm. From the rear Joe called, "Mother, stop! Nig's load is slipping!"

Slipping! In another moment the precious pack of fruit would have been on the rocks. Nig was stopped dead, his feet braced. So I got off and squatted at his side to decide what to do, while Nig rolled his eye at me.

If I worked at the dangling packbox and a corner tickled his belly, he would lash out with his feet until he smashed everything and tangled himself in the ropes besides.

"Oh Mother, be careful!" Patsy implored, turning to look at the eastern ridges glittering in the last sun, and the creeping shadows on this unfamiliar hillside. If anything happened, this would be a most scary place to spend the night.

"Patsy, you hold Nig's rope and talk to him," I said. "Be ready to jump if you have to. Joe, you take Steve and keep out of the way."

Standing on the high side of the trail I could reach the hitch on the packsaddle, but I would never be able to replace the load and make it ride. As I moved around Nig at a safe distance he continued to watch me. A mule is very curious about human beings.

If I moved abruptly, twitches rippled the hair on his side, and he quivered in general with deviltry. Patsy was saying over and over, "Nig, look this way. Look at Patsy!"

Loosening the knot, I inched the pack down until it lay intact on the ground. This was Nig's chance, and he rippled a little more to show he was aware of it. I went around him, speaking so he would know where I was; I stooped; I drew the box out of his way, never taking my eyes from his rear hoofs.

Whereupon he rested a hind leg indolently and closed his eyes. I loosed the two cinches and put the saddle in position. When I tightened the first cinch, Nig groaned, out of habit. Joe and Steve had watched in anxious silence. Now I said, "Everything's fine. Everybody up."

Joe climbed on, and I heaved Steve up to ride behind Patsy. I took Nig's rope, mounted my own horse, and we were off. Probably nothing but a bear would bother the fruit we were leaving behind; we'd have to risk that.

We had been in camp barely an hour when Len arrived afoot, with the abandoned huckleberries tied somehow to his riding saddle. He had found no strayed sheep; all was well.

I was making supper in the lantern-lit tent, and he came and stood by my shoulder. "So you lost your load," he teased. "Maybe you'd better learn to throw a hitch. I've seen several women do it. Celia Titus is a wonderful packer. Maybe a woman is worth more if she can pack!"

"I should think she would be," I said. "Worth a lot more!"

For this interval we had fun. Life seemed unbelievably gay and easy, and I kept the cookshack at Little Bar sealed in a closed compartment of my mind. Here on the mountain I had no housekeeping, and only the plainest cooking to do. Yet we could have the herders in to a dinner that they thought wonderful because someone else cooked it, a dinner that ended with the same huckleberry cobbler and canned milk day after day. This, for some reason, was the dessert of which they never tired.

We could read magazines and play horseshoes. The kids and I helped Len on the plywood grubboxes he had designed, boxes that would angle *around* the mule's sides instead of riding awkwardly tangent. We helped saw up a fallen tree, Len at his end pitted against four of us in relays at the other end of the saw.

Dick came to camp reporting that he had been sick at the ranch, with no one but Mr. Russell to look after him. He was still frightened, and his swollen ankles proved he must have had a serious attack of some kind. After a few hours he left, seeming more self-possessed but quite vague as to when he would return to the ranch, or whether he would go in at all now. Obviously this was not the time to open a discussion about the future.

Our summer was done, and we must get back to the ranch and to *problems*. So we packed our canned berries and left for Grangeville. In a new auto camp with hot showers and good beds, Len and I had one last evening of luxury together.

My husband began: "Kirkwood will not divide. I've thought it out, and to do the only kind of job I'm interested in doing, we need it all. It will not cut into two satisfactory units. We could move our family to the Carter house and live by ourselves. That might make everything better, and if you didn't have a garden to tend and men to cook for, you could teach the children yourself. We could order that home-instruction course you were telling me about."

Mentally I checked Carter Mansion. No phone. A long way from the boat landing. The down-in-a-crack location of the house. I would be staring all day at nothing but rocky ridges just outside the windows, with only a shoestring of field on one side for relief. Well, I thought, other women had probably lived in a crack and survived.

"Get off a letter about the Calvert course before you start to the ranch," Len urged.

Kirkwood had never looked so good nor seemed so naturally ours to have and to hold. Mr. Russell had kept things up and even canned tomatoes for me, but there were still quantities of the big red ones, and neighbors on the divide were phoning to ask if they could get some. The last cucumbers were ready for pickling, and the ground-cherries rustled in their paper shells. Big bald squashes peered out of their dry, hairy vines, but the watermelons were gone and those strange *round* melons, Mr. Russell complained, weren't going to ripen at all!

"Those are citron," I said. "Murrielle brought us a citron last year, and I saved the seeds. Wait until you get a jar of the preserves."

"Citron preserves!" Mr. Russell was a bit aggravated to hear of a kind of preserves he had never encountered.

"Citron preserves," I repeated.

In the yard and in the new little clearing across the creek, my young walnut trees were doing well, and the peach trees we had set below the crossing had summered nicely. The grain hay, sowed this year to rest the soil, was now stubble, and it spread a gold aura around the potato patch set in its midst. They were the first potatoes we had raised

—big,—beautiful ones now almost ready for digging.

The youngberry planting I had made in the wornout strawberry ground had done so well it should bear next year. And sweetest of all, the tiny lawn spaded and leveled by my hand alone, was still green, thanks to Mr. Russell, and as soothing as Patsy's bed of seven-foot double hollyhocks.

First the canning and preserving must be finished, then there would be one last crop to harvest, the walnuts. With crisp weather the first nuts would come tumbling down, and late each afternoon we would gather them to store in our low attic. To go from tree to tree, searching in the rustling leaves for the last vagrant nut, was pure pleasure. The squirrels watched, wondering about their share; and passers-by stopped to fill their pockets.

Everything was beautiful, even though we knew that all this was tentative.

As partnerships often do, ours came to an end. When given his choice, Dick declined either to buy or to sell. Nor would he consider our moving to the Carter house. But he had no counter plan, and the impasse must be resolved.

We were forced to bid high, and when I learned the figure, and the amount of our first payment a year hence, I was terrified, yet I knew the risk Len was taking for us was calculated—minutely calculated. However, there was this to be kept in mind every waking hour: if we failed on the first installment we should lose Kirkwood and with it four years of the hardest labor Len and I had ever known.

Dick came to the ranch a few months after the settlement, but just to get his things. He stayed only until the boat went up the river and returned.

# 8

WE SAT AT THE KITCHEN TABLE, AND LEN EXAMINED the notes he always kept on operation costs. He put down an estimate of what next spring's wool might bring, assuming that production and marketing conditions did not change radically; then, the income from lambs and aged ewes a year hence on the same basis. Now he went over the cost of supplemental feeds, wages, boat freight, range fees, and the expense of boarding herders in camp and hired men at the ranch, regularly and seasonally. When he had added everything and allowed for replacements and depreciation and a further margin for the unforeseeable, it was clear that to make the payment next October we would have to hold our personal spending to the absolute minimum.

"You'll have to do on twenty-five dollars a month," my husband announced.

"You mean for clothes, medicines, reading matter, insurance, vacations, and the children's school courses?" I asked slowly.

"Yes. But you've already got the school courses paid for. Nothing will be due on them for a year, and with this re-use arrangement you can make, the cost next time will drop."

"Well," I explained, "there is, actually, another fee. I've discovered that my payment covered only the books, materials and instruction manual, not the criticism. Still, I imagine we could do nicely without the criticism. After all I've taught grade school," I said importantly.

"Better send more money," Len advised. "Don't skip anything essential."

He was right. When the grades and comment came back from the Calvert School concerning our first test lessons, I almost wept. The work I had sent in so proudly was labeled "untidy, inexact, formless,"—in fact, "below standard." Promptly I sent the criticism fee and we raised our sights.

The explicit manual and materials were a delight. So too was the general plan. Almost from the beginning, history, geography and art were interrelated. The story of nations was not confined to wars and kings, but encompassed national ideals, religion, architecture and other fine arts. In time, the physical world, the heavens and the limiting seas would be related to the picture, and before many months passed a pupil would be putting down his orderly if ambitious gleanings, and the result would be an English paper.

Handwriting, as the simplest evidence of the child's labor, was important past belief. It must be almost as plain as print. Sweaty little hands must make letters that stayed rigidly on lines and fitted into definite spaces. Low letters must observe a single ceiling; looped letters rose higher or dropped lower, but also had precise bounds. The writing Patsy and Joe had learned last year must be abandoned at once—and remaking a hand would be no simpler for them than it would be for an adult.

Ruler-drawn margins on four sides of the arithmetic papers were law. Examples must be further sequestered between horizontal lines, ruler drawn. No crowding, no piling, no running up or down hill would be excused.

We were colliding, head on, with a new science.

From the first day of school it was clear that only by setting a rigid program would we ever protect ourselves from the double threat of alien interruptions and our own natural inertia. Therefore we outlined a daily schedule.

After breakfast Patsy and I cleared the table, then while I prepared vegetables or made pies, she washed the dishes and Joe wiped them. The rule changed only when the breakfast crowd rose above eight, a fixed number. With the dishes done, my scholars had leisure for their own pursuits while I made beds and put the kitchen in order. Meanwhile, someone had brought in the milk, which must be strained and set in the cellar, after which the bucket and strainer must be washed and scalded.

By eight-thirty we were ready for school, and on dark mornings we began by the light of the Rochester lamp. If the weather was bad, Steve amused himself with crayons or paper cutting. If he went outside, he must remain within call. At recess he was put down for a nap and we were rid of him for the rest of the morning—there was no afternoon session.

We began classes the week after Thanksgiving, and it was soon evident that my idea of doing fancy work or writing letters during school hours was quite naive. Neither child could work long alone, not if he was to earn Calvert praise. At best, I could keep beans boiling, or a pot roast simmering. At eleven-thirty we closed, and from then until twelve I rushed like mad to get dinner on the table.

Strangers and unconvinced neighbors gave us something of a problem. If they decided against knocking at the door, they would be squatting just outside, rolling cigarettes while they waited for noon. If it was raining, I had to go out and suggest that they make a fire in the bunkhouse. Some callers entered with the merest tap on the door and proceeded to "visit," on the assumption that this was expected of one who aimed to stay for dinner. The bent heads and earnest expressions of the children at the table did not convey to the visitor that Silence was reigning.

Once in the midst of a morning storm, an old gentleman blew in, on business that was still vague when he left. At the moment, Mr. Mason's hands were blue and his nose ready to drip, so I put him in a chair by the range. And when he declared he had participated in the history of the region and had known people who were attacked by the Nez Perces in 1877, I halted school so the children could talk to him. But as history his tales proved to be long on prejudice and confused as to dates.

After examining Mr. Mason's thin gray thatch with a somewhat disappointed air Joe asked, "The Indians didn't scalp you, did they?"

Steve laid a hand on the visitor's steaming knee and the old gentleman pulled him to a seat there. "What are you good for?" the visitor asked.

Steve fingered Mr. Mason's veiny cheek curiously. "I'm good to kiss," he said, then thought better of this statement and jumped hastily down.

On another morning old John, who was working in the

fields at Big Bar, limped in during lessons and announced, "I'd like my breakfast please."

John had a good camp with plenty of supplies. He was a faithful old ship, rusty but uncomplaining, and he had never before asked an unreasonable favor. So I pushed back basic spelling and Greek Myths and set him a meal as fast as I could cook it.

On still another morning a lambing hand walked in the door without knocking. Before seating himself he turned on the phonograph, and when I firmly turned it off, he said in a mild way, "I just wanted to see if it worked."

After the noon dishes were done, the children were free; and later I had my one sure moment in the open, when I crossed the creek to feed the chickens and gather the eggs. If there was still time I took the kids to the river, merely to scramble around among the boulders and see what we could see. There were always interesting tracks at the water's edge, and other surprises if the river was high, for the Snake had already made its way for hundreds of miles, collecting tribute as it ran. Once a whole staircase floated by. Bridge timbers with great bolts were not uncommon, and in flood time, trees with terrifying roots hurtled down, sometimes diving under, then shooting out of the boiling tide further below, ejected by some unseen force.

Before supper the two boys brought wood, and Patsy set the table. There was as yet no *home work,* and after supper the children could do as they pleased until bedtime, but this came early for us all. Breakfast would be on by seven, often by six, and no one, simply no one, ever slept in.

Patsy was obliged to toil hard, for she was plunged into a demanding new system with no chance to learn the Calvert fundamentals that Joe was getting. Her Baltimore critic let us examine the papers of day-school pupils, and we saw we were in no danger of trying too hard. Our unseen mentors showed warm interest, and it was edifying to find that their letters were prepared with the same stern exactness they demanded of pupils.

Christmas was now only a few weeks away, and already the excitement and secrecy had begun. Patsy had been making tea towels; Joe did calendars. For some of their relatives they had to buy modest presents. Each child had an allowance, and in my account book a page. He received a check once a year, which was deposited for him in the savings bank, but at all times his credit was assumed to be good, and he could shop by way of the mail-order catalogues, one of us parents writing the order after a sober conference. The amount of the child's purchase was charged in the book against his year's allowance, and even the postage was charged if he insisted on his order coming singly.

Ordinarily, to please the mail-order people, all packages arrived under one name, mine. So when it came time for the children to buy a present for me, it was necessary to conspire. Subsequently a large aluminum teakettle, with modern, heat-proof off-center handle, was shipped to someone in the bunkhouse. Sometimes when I didn't see the kids around, they were in the old cabin, examining and fondling that wonderful kettle, ready to shove the box under the bed at any sound.

Patsy was aware now that Santa was only a spun-sugar delight, but she loved perpetuating him for Steve and Joe. In the catalogue she helped Joe find a Boy Scout hatchet, and for his English paper he was allowed to compose a note addressed properly to Santa Claus, North Pole, stating that he would like a hatchet like the one on page 673 of

Sears Roebuck, but that something else would be fine if he was asking for too much.

Len and I agreed to give ourselves one gift, a radio, and I wondered mournfully if we could really afford it. We had never owned a good battery set, and at this moment thirty dollars seemed a tremendous sum. Nevertheless we splurged. As usual, the boat before Christmas brought numerous packages for the children. Our friends and kin did not seem to know about the depression. Page Hosmer had sent her annual big box.

However, the early hours on Christmas day were once again hollow, for the children and I were by ourselves. We knew that Len would be struggling with his packstring along some snowy ridge in the gray depths of the sky. He could not start home until he had set up a new camp and left the herder a supply of firewood, drinking water, and whatever else he would need.

But by two o'clock, my husband came stamping into the house, and Mr. Russell had already arrived—with gifts. When dinner was served, we could repeat the Christmas grace together and feel we were indeed blessed and fortunate.

When the day waned and radio reception picked up, we turned on the new Silvertone, and it was an arresting thing to have the great Christmas music come flooding into our low-ceilinged kitchen. To this day, carol singing or "The Messiah" takes me back to the house at Kirkwood.

Outside, the snow was deepening, and Mr. Russell must start home before total blackness enveloped his private trail along the cliffs. When Len had finished the chores, he tenderly transported to the poultry house a silly old biddy. She had taken refuge from the snow in a keg of nails by the forge, a very unsafe place on a winter night. Len hated hens as much as ever, but the Christmas spirit is invincible.

Snug in the lamplight we ended our day. At bedtime, when Joe said his prayers, I saw the handle of the new hatchet under his pillow. Santa had been able to find among his stores the one that was exactly right. Joe's only trouble would be keeping it away from his father.

Through the anxious months ahead, the radio was a great solace to me. Since the batteries must be conserved, we indulged in no serial dramas, but early in the morning and again at night we had a newscast. Every Sunday evening we listened to a program that we remembered all the next week. This program was Major Bowes' Amateur Hour.

If Len was at home, I put everything else aside, and for that one hour, we sat together at the top of the dark stairs, where the radio occupied an improvised stand. At that time the major used a gong to indicate disapproval, and the gong could be very cruel. We felt—at least I did—that only a few feet away were those who contended, like us, against unforeseeable and perhaps unjust odds. However, the major's protégés would know with merciful speed whether they had done well or ill. Our answer was months away.

The children were bored by the major, and unless we insisted on their listening, they went about their own affairs. But on the stairway Len and I listened to the major's impelling voice, held his hand and each other's, and were protected for that hour by a wall of warmth and darkness from the harsh realities of life.

Mr. Russell, who was much in demand along the river as a choreman, hay hand and telephone repairer, had agreed to come to Kirkwood and stay as long as he would be needed. Though the bunkhouse was well supplied with quilts and wool blankets, he brought his own; and I gave him sheets and pillow cases. Before moving in he insisted on cleaning and tidying the place until it looked garnished, at least through the middle. No one knew exactly what lay on the top shelves of the open cupboards flanking the boarded-up fireplace, but there would certainly be ammunition for firearms old and new, broken spurs and parts of guns, nails, a branding iron or two, the insides of old phonographs, rat traps, broken alarm clocks, maybe some dynamite caps—altogether a dusty, fascinating hoard. David Kirk had died in this room; babies had been born in it. But because preachers were a rarity in the canyon, it probably had seen no weddings.

Of course Mr. Russell would have to share the bunkhouse at times with other men, and when he found one of them merely *seated* on his bed he was affronted. If some imbecile left a fresh coyote pelt or a sweaty saddle blanket there, Mr. Russell almost blew himself apart.

Regularly on Sunday morning, and to make up in a way for church services, he hiked down to his cabin to make sure that during the week his kingdom had not been violated. He took a bath in his washtub, wrote to his sister, and no doubt communed with his soul. Returning, he always seemed like something fresh-made, and seeing this I wished that I could command a similar little island in time.

Mr. Russell despised sheep—he said—and never touched one. Certainly he classed himself as superior to lambing help, and he enjoyed alluding to people who were "anxious to get out of the sheep business into something higher." But when it came to gardening or tinkering usefully all day long, he had no equal; and his eternal busyness was the more astonishing when you observed his spare frame, which seemed entirely composed of bones and tendons.

This spring we looked toward lambing with special intensity, for we were eager to see any improvement in our Rambouillet strain that might be attributed to the nine Hampshire bucks Len had put with the ewes in November. They had cost twenty dollars apiece, a shocking price in 1935.

It was also this spring that Al Reynolds came. A quiet man of forty or so, with a mild blue gaze and a patient manner, he was a pleasure to have around; for Al listened and weighed his words before he spoke, and he spoke but seldom. He read everything serious that came to his hand, and he could tell you what Mark Hanna said in 1903, and explain Bryan's Free Silver theory without subscribing to it. He had attended college and been a business man, but he herded sheep because he minded solitude very little, very much less than he minded some people and their town ways. He missed his wife and children, but it was necessary for them to be near a high school.

Mrs. Reynolds had consented to help us during lambing and shearing, so that I should not have to stop school so much; and one morning Eagle was dispatched across the divide to fetch her in.

I first saw Jessie Reynolds as she dismounted in her bib overalls. She was large, a neat woman, with her hair in a dark curly bob, and for all her riding that spring she would wear these same overalls, changing to the prettiest of dresses the moment she was established under a roof. There was no place on the range that she was unwilling to go, provided she could have Eagle. She held to the belief that any intelligent horse knew more about trails than she did; and on a bad ledge she never dismounted nor allowed herself to get tense. Let the horse worry; that was his business.

Her presence was a blessing. Even after lambing began I could work in the garden right up to breakfast time, because

Mrs. Reynolds would have it on the table. And on any afternoon I could do a big washing, instead of waiting until the always hectic weekend.

Lambing began favorably, for Len had been able to call in his best help of the previous spring, men who knew and liked his system and who appreciated the way we fed and regarded our hired men. The isolation itself lured a few to the canyon, at least for a few weeks of good pay. They could go home afterward and be as mysterious as they pleased, and their wives would have no means of checking up on them.

"Marking" is the final indication of the year's program of breeding, herding and lambing. It is, however, a nervous, bloody business, best done on a cool or rainy day. All lambs' tails are cut off, and their ears are notched to show age and ownership. In addition, the wether (male) lambs are castrated. The count, when all is over, is a percentage—the percent of live lambs to ewes, and the ewes must include the "drys," and those that for any reason have no lamb at their side. In the canyon, with open-range lambing, one-hundred-fifty percent was a legendary figure. We felt fortunate with an average among our bands of one hundred twenty-four; and that inexorable day in the coming autumn made the marking figure terribly important.

After two weeks on the river, Mrs. Reynolds handed her bags to the packer, mounted Eagle from a stout box, and was borne from our sight. She would be moving from one short-time camp to another as the grass improved on the higher slopes, always following the drop-band upward. The bough beds the packer would build for her would never be very soft, and she would cook on a tin stove in a small tent, with only a few more cooking utensils than a herder usually had. Her only advantages were pre-knowledge of what she was getting into, and her own cheerful temperament. In addition to being good natured, Mrs. Reynolds had a reputation for turning out superb food under the meagerest conditions.

Her boarders would not be limited to men on our payroll. Let a woman and a skillet assemble at the most inaccessible spot in the canyon, and hungry men will flock there. The word goes from ridge to ridge, like smoke signals; and with the most transparent of excuses, men will ride in and wait around for the mess call, squatting to roll cigarettes, never growing impatient.

When the meal is finally served and over—and they may have had to eat it standing—they will "wait for the boss" unless told firmly that he isn't expected and couldn't possibly come. With any encouragement they will stretch their stay past another meal, or over night.

It is all nonsense that to attract men a woman must be evil, exotic, or even curvy. Endow her with good nature, supply her with groceries, and men will come a-running. You cannot keep them away with clubs. No woman ever came into the canyon single and remained so except by her own choice and by employing main strength.

At the ranch too we were always favored with spring visitors. They were of many sorts: actual neighbors riding somewhere on business; passengers from the boat; men ostensibly hunting for work; and a final group that resisted classification. It included runaway teen-age boys, shifty-mannered men who had no tale to tell and whom we tried to feed and speed on their way, agreeable representatives of livestock credit corporations, prospectors, deputy sheriffs, deputy assessors, conservation and game officials, scientific "bug" men and geologists, and the ever-welcome Forest Service employees. In one month that spring I set seventy-eight meals for people who were not of our household or on our payroll.

We accepted no money, but the Forest men continued to leave bills on the table. Of the rest many were grateful and we wished they would come again. Now and then, it was true, someone "ordered" a dish expecting that he would be allowed to pay. Some objected to our never-failing cooked breakfast cereal until they saw that it was served with whipped cream.

Often next week's mail brought a little present for the children. Once some delightful medical excursionists from Spokane, who had stopped for beds and breakfast, sent me Gibran's *The Prophet*.

There was one visitor that I did not expect to see again. During the winter Jake Gaus had received a summons, not the summons of death but of more light. He appeared at the house one morning in considerable excitement, explaining that his religious sect had called him to come to Los Angeles, and he did not have the money to make the trip.

He did not know precisely how he was to serve, and he was not disturbed by the thought of the vast difference between the silent canyon and the roaring ant hill of life in so great a city. He only knew he had been called and must go.

"I want to sell you everything I've got," he finished.

Len was away at the time and I hardly felt equal, on my own, to buying out Jake, especially as I had never been to his place. But at least I could explore the problem.

"What does your outfit include and what do you want for it?" I asked.

He listed his assets. Besides the motto-papered cabin and its furnishings, he had mining equipment, and this included many tools that would be useful even though they duplicated things we already had. He mentioned his canned fruit, and I was in no doubt as to what I would do with that.

"I need twenty dollars," he finished, "so that's what I want for it all."

I told him when to come back again, and that he could count on the money, but why not regard it as a loan? He could repay us when he returned to the canyon later, and we would give him back all his things.

"I'll never return," he explained, "as long as I am still getting more light."

So Jake went out on the next boat, and beyond a couple of penny postals written in red ink and consisting largely of scripture, we heard no more of him.

Shearing time had come again. As before, we had arranged with Kenneth Johnson to have the one crew shear both outfits. The crew would come in by boat, finish Kenneth's sheep first, then cross to us at Little Bar. With a prearranged price per head the crew was assured enough work to justify the long boat trip in; and one portable engine was sufficient for both plants. We could also exchange wrangling help; and thoughtful Hazel offered us space in her kerosene refrigerator for our fresh meat.

A few days in advance of shearing Mrs. Reynolds rejoined us, and together we packed huge boxes of groceries, fruit, preserves, canned meat, bedding, dish towels, hand towels, oil lamps and lanterns, dishes, wash basins, washtubs, water cans and over-size cooking utensils.

A special order of bread and green vegetables from Mrs. Sapp's Grocery in Lewiston would come on the last possible boat, and would be taken on to Little Bar for unloading. But if rain fell on Kenneth, and the crew had to be held there unduly long, our fresh food would be past using.

Old John dropped his work to go to Little Bar as Mrs. Reynolds' helper. Ignoring his stiff knee, he would carry wood and water, wash dishes and prepare vegetables all day long. And by the time the shearers set foot on the rocks at Little Bar he would have cleaned the cookshack and stone cellar so that everything would be ready to start feeding them.

Then came five hectic, driving, steaming days in the sun-warped plant, to the rumble of the engine and the roll of the long shaft, to the yelling of the sheep wranglers and the piercing cries of lambs separated from their mothers. But finally the engine slowed to a stop, the shearers disengaged their clippers, and the nearly naked wool-tromper climbed out of his suspended sack and rubbed his oily brown back with a rag. Shearing was over now and our worries were a thing of the past.

While the horses drew the four-hundred pound bags of wool to the landing and the crew gathered its belongings, Len checked the men's tallies. The boat arrived, and from the bar the human exodus began, while up the hot ridges streamed the scrawny-looking ewes and their still anguished lambs.

Mrs. Reynolds helped the packer dismantle the cookshack and before the day's end they were on their way with the packstring toward Kirkwood. Except for the piled wool, of which the *Chief* had been able to take only a part, the trampled corrals, and the littered spots where the shearers' tents had stood, Little Bar slept in the sun as lonely as before.

On Kenneth Johnson it had rained, though not enough to delay him much since he had shelter for many sheep. On us it had not rained at all, and viewing nature's favoritism and other good fortune which had befallen us, Kenneth and Hazel named Len "Lucky Jordan." He did not mind.

He had contracted our wool by telephone at twenty-seven cents, a nice price in 1936.

For yet another day Kirkwood teemed with people. Then

Mrs. Reynolds caught the special wool boat, and our extra men took their checks and left, afoot or by horse, to cross the divide to the Salmon. Only Mr. Russell remained at the ranch, and a crushed feeling came upon the children and me. In another two or three weeks, depending on when the Forest Service declared the summer range open, Len would start the bands to high pasture. Then solitude would really encompass the ranch.

Since school began, just after Thanksgiving, we had lost only a few days, but with June holding a burning-glass over the canyon and July sure to be equally hot, we strove to finish the lesson units we were on and stop. Next year, if there was a next year, Steve's mornings should include work as well as play. He would be four years old and he could begin the kindergarten course the Calvert School offered.

Being of lively mind, he needed part of his time planned for him. I had already been obliged to show him the difference between mishaps he could foresee and those he could not. Foreseeable ones were less forgivable than the other sort. Clearly he found it rather entertaining to provoke mild sputtering and dismay in adults; and the hours before his morning nap were a tempting period.

On the idea of his joining school the older children looked with no great relish, but I explained that Steve would have a table to himself and not get in their way.

# 9

BEFORE WE COULD TAKE OUR ANNUAL TRIP OUT, THERE was one project that should be completed, the securing of a safe and satisfactory supply of domestic water. The kitchen faucet was a big brass affair of unknown ancestry, and the water was piped down to it at lively pressure from the irrigation ditch. A hundred yards above the house this ditch emerged from the creek, skirted a cliff, cut through a trail, and flowed around the base of a steep rise to reach the yard. For drinking purposes the water might have been boiled, but it never was.

When the men irrigated the south field, the pipe to the house ceased to run, and if the faucet was thoughtlessly left open, trouble was bound to result after the irrigating was finished.

One afternoon as I picked raspberries, Steve strolled by, happy and casual. He paused to chatter a while, then remarked that "some water was running."

"Where?" I asked, without stopping work.

"In the kitchen," he said.

"Well, is it doing any harm?" I asked, continuing to pick.

The little boy appeared to be weighing my exact meaning, and then as if finally satisfied he said, "It's kind of running out of the sink."

My sub-level kitchen floor! I tossed away my pail, bolted the barbed wire fence, and flew. From the rim of the sink, water was indeed running. It creamed in a wide sheet, the linoleum was already floating up where it could, and across the threshold into the dirt-floored cellar a tide was lapping softly.

I splashed through to close the tap, then cried to the other children to help. With basins and buckets we bailed madly, and the level began to drop. Half an hour later, with a final mopping, we had done all we could. Given time, the cellar would take care of itself, but for days the kitchen would breathe a miasma of mold.

This unpleasant event could easily happen over and over. So Len talked to Mr. Russell, who was an expert on plumbing as well as on the operation of telephonic communication and the production of band music. Mr. Russell went with me to examine a small spring that rose from under a cliff near the first bend in the trail and presently lost itself in the creek. If this spring was reamed out and a wooden box with a low-level outlet was sunk in it, cold, clean water could be piped under the creek and down to the house. The buried pipe would be cool in summer and reasonably frost-free in winter.

So ditch-digging was added to Mr. Russell's long day, and though he regarded this work as no compliment to his more artistic and technical skills, he began the task graciously. After a couple of weeks he called me to see the plank box with hinged lid which he had set in place in the spring. Looking down through the green depths, I found the screened outlet, already connected with the ground pipe.

"She's ready to go!" Mr. Russell announced with triumph. "And when I hook the pipe to your sink tap, I'll leave you an outside faucet. Then you can screw on a hose and keep your lawn wet. It don't take much water just to *encourage* grass."

The water system added immensely to our sense of permanence. Also it would please Len's mother, a woman who worried considerably about germs, her own and other people's.

Through July Len rushed to the ranch whenever he could be away from the sheep camps. But after he had finished the second crop of hay and I had the apricots in jars, we would have a little time for leisure.

For the summer we had turned over our bucks to Dick Carter, who ran a farm flock of his own. Even in their short summer fleeces, our bucks suffered miseries in the river heat. Sometimes they took refuge in old mine entrances, and in such hiding places they could not be found for counting, yet they were still not safe from roaming cougars, who were bold enough to attack even a horse.

Dick Carter understood a buck's mind, and this was important. Bucks love battle, and unless handled right they will tear up a stout wire enclosure. With their cumbersome horns a pair will fight each other to a standstill, and the sight of blood and the crash of bone on bone drive the timid bucks into combat too. The contest goes on until the lesser bucks are all exhausted, and the last two on their feet battle it out. But Dick understood them, and his pastures were high and temperate, with covers of green timber. So our bucks were in the best of hands.

We were resolved not to spoil the summer with worry, and at this point there was only one thing left to do anyhow, to bring out the most lambs and the fattest lambs possible. Again we went to Pilot Rock.

In the trap was a black bear, but it was a small creature that one could hardly hate. Ben Beaudry had baited the trap with the carcasses of lambs the bear had killed wantonly after satisfying its hunger. Though it was an ignoble rascal, and a killer, the bear was not a happy sight on the thrashed earth, and I could not rest until Ben had finished it off.

It was the children's first bear and they studied it intently, especially its padded feet and the toe-dented round tracks it had left. At the ranch they knew many different tracks—the small peppered impressions, each with trailing quill lines, made by porcupines on their nightly rounds; the tender prints like baby hands of coons looking for a ripe melon. Coons were worse than porcupines, for they were death on hens. Let a silly hen hide in a tree after dark, and her red comb and stripped bones might be dangling there next morning.

Coyote tracks could be confused with dog tracks, except by those who knew and mistrusted coyotes. These foxy fellows liked to sit on a ridge at moonrise and mock their frantic cousins, the ranch dogs below.

Bobcat, mink and otter tracks were all visible at times along the river. Deer tracks were especially exciting to the children. They could picture the nervous creatures slipping into the fields under cover of darkness to feast on planted crops, their big ears and eyes alert for danger. Deer tracks and sheep tracks are somewhat alike—the spacing tells the story, for the actual movements of deer and sheep are as different as their natures. As different as quicksilver and jam.

Grandma and Grandpa arrived for a week's visit at camp. With their presence as an excuse, we explored the Forest Service roads and the old mining camps of the region. We visited the look-outs, and the decaying Mountain House, where in the old days freighters between Lewiston and Buffalo Hump had stopped over night. The depth of those winter snows was indicated by the old tree stumps standing six and eight feet above the ground. Now the mines were mostly abandoned, and only the deep trenches of forgotten roads, or such ruins as the Mountain House, remained.

During his grandparents' visit Steve addressed his father one morning, possibly for dramatic effect: "Daddy, are we still poor?"

"Poor!" my husband's mother cried in horror.

I explained that by "poor" Steve did not mean "destitute," for he had never seen destitute people. To him "poor" meant having to make overalls last as long as possible—also crayons, fishline, toys, and shoes. And on that basis the answer to his question was "Yes."

"He shouldn't know what 'poor' means!" Grandma insisted.

"Oh yes he should," I said, "and it hasn't made him very sad, do you think?"

Our vacation was over, and I was not sorry to be going to the river, though in bad moments I wondered if it would be our last going-home. It was late in August now, so Len could not take time to go in with us. A strange man brought the horses to meet us at the deserted mill site on Cow Creek.

He seemed harmless enough and I soon found he had been merely looking over the canyon, was a friend of a friend, and had volunteered to bring the horses over.

Sheepmen, as contrasted with cattlemen, never ride faster than a steady walk, and this measured pace through a vast, unpeopled landscape encourages reflection. As we rode, I thought back over the year. We had planned and operated with all the efficiency we possessed; we had spared no physical effort; and whether it profited us or not, we had done a good deal of worrying, both aloud to each other, and in secret. In the management of the ranch we had stopped a good many leaks.

If we could make this first payment, we could handle the others, which were smaller and would be spread. As soon as we knew what the lambs would bring, we would know whether our four years work had bought us a ranch and some sharp experience, or only the latter.

Time was growing short. When the lamb buyers arrived in Grangeville, Len must be there to contact them. Buyers to whom we had sold before knew what to expect in our lambs, and thus the deal should be somewhat less of a gamble; yet buyers must respect the country-wide market or lose their own shirts, and the market had been known to fluctuate widely within the space of a few hours. Regardless of what the lambs brought, and what this meant to our future, the sheep must be trailed to railhead on the Clearwater, the lambs and aged ewes must be cut out, and then the breeding stock started toward the ranch.

Though I began school as if I expected to go on teaching all winter and for years to come, I listened by day and by night for the phone, which had now been moved down to the kitchen. At lessons the older children swung into line competently; for brief periods they could even follow their manuals unaided, and I could give my time to Steve.

When he first opened the magic boxes that were a part of the kindergarten course, there were longing eyes at the other table. Here were colored sticks, shoe pegs, wooden beads, lentils, sewing cards, bright construction paper and gay weaving materials. But there were words and meanings to learn too, as Len was to see the first time he came home. Reproving Steve for some small mistake in judgment, Len said goodnaturedly: "Steve, I don't believe you know straight up!"

"Yes, I do," Steve said carefully. "Straight up is *vuhtical.* When it is level, you must say *hoh-izontal.*"

But now Grangeville was calling. Len's voice came in clearly, and I stopped breathing and held my heart.

He spoke in the quiet tone that had never failed to comfort me, even in some very bad moments. "The lambs," he said distinctly, "brought eight cents, which is more than we counted on. Everything is going to be okay. But I can't come in now. And as soon as I get the lambs trailed and shipped, I'll leave directly for Portland."

Leaving for Portland meant just one thing, seeing our bankers. There were no financial Santa Clauses in 1936, not in the ranch and livestock business. Banks still foreclosed and tragic people still had to ask for "relief." We ourselves had attempted a stiff commitment, and made it. But we would need expense money for a while, and credit institutions did not choose their clients by reading tea leaves or consulting astrologers. They required evidence in the shape of records and estimates.

I had no one to tell my good news to, and nothing concrete to tell. Everybody on the phone line would already know what we had got for the lambs. So I told the children only that Dad was fine but it would be many more days before he was home. I think we celebrated the lamb sale by making a trip around through the cliffs to Halfmoon and playing for an hour on the sandbar there.

When at last Len came home, the autumn had gone from golden to frosty, and it was the most brisk and exciting time of the year in the canyon, a fall to remember and treasure. Not only had the Portland conference been financially satisfactory, but Len had spent hours with other stockmen, wool men, and heads of credit agencies who had their own slant on the future of livestock and agriculture under a runaway government.

As for our bankers, their sympathy and imagination seemed to have been seized by Len's reports and sound estimates, together with his plans for meeting new situations that might develop. Perhaps they even wondered if a sheep ranch in Snake Canyon mightn't be a pretty good place for a man to batten down and ride out the depression. In any event their final word to Len was to go ahead, that he had their confidence.

So we felt gayer now than for a long, long time, and we were in a mood to celebrate. But going out of the canyon for frivolity was neither practicable nor in Jordan style. We preferred to get together with our neighbors.

On a November day it would be possible to bring to our isolated bar only a few of the neighbors who, regardless of our different pattern of ranching and of living, had shown their confidence in our intentions and our ability these four years. But here was Thanksgiving almost at hand, so what about a houseparty for those who could come?

First on the list were any and all bachelors within riding distance; then our nearest and most-visited neighbors, the

Kenneth Johnsons. And across the divide were the Don Axtells, and on Cow Creek the Slim Johnsons.

The McGaffee families had moved into Oregon and the Hibbses were too far away, so we could expect none of them. And the Jack Tituses from Pittsburg Landing had wide family connections and would be celebrating in a big way themselves.

All our prospective guests were delighted, all except the Kenneth Johnsons who said they had planned a holiday outside the canyon. However, Hazel Johnson sent me two young turkeys as a Thanksgiving gift, and since the boat was now running we could have the traditional side dishes of Thanksgiving, such comparative luxuries as oysters for the dressing, fresh cranberries, olives, celery and lettuce.

Monday morning ushered in a freeze, followed by steady dry snow, and amid my full-steam preparations I had to admit that with stormy weather, my party might fall quite flat.

But on Tuesday Don Axtell phoned that they would make the trip the day *before* Thanksgiving, so as to cross the divide with their two small children during the warmest part of the day. Slim and Mary Johnson had farther to come, but it would take a blizzard to hold them back. As for the widowers, Dick Carter and Till Phillips, they would make it if anyone could.

Wednesday afternoon was turning gray along its edges when Fanny and Belle rushed out to announce strange horses approaching; and round the bend in the Kirkwood trail came the Axtells. Don dismounted with the blanketed baby asleep in his arms, saying it had been cold on top of the pass but not very windy. When he lifted Larry down from behind his mother, the child was too stiff to stand. He was not yet three, and though he must have ached cruelly with the cold, he did not as much as whimper.

We took the guests in, and when they had eaten a hot snack and toasted themselves at the range, they seemed to feel quite at home. As dusk closed down and the fires and lamps burned brighter, Len came home and we felt as if Thanksgiving was already beginning.

Don and Frances Axtell were unlike most people in the region, being neither natives of the hills nor new ranchers. In fact they were not ranchers at all. They were college graduates who had come from the east with a dream. They wanted to find freedom from the class-consciousness and conventional thinking with which they had grown up. Frances had seen the Snake-Salmon divide before she married Don, and he had succumbed to her tales of it.

They had secured a small mountain-side tract with a view of the ridgy country far beyond the Salmon; and here Don had built a log cabin that could be reached by trail only. Don was trained in electrical engineering, for which there was no demand on the divide, so when he needed money he worked at whatever he could find to do—such as helping us through lambing.

Meanwhile the Axtells raised a garden, got out logs, read omnivorously, and took delight in the natives. They were rearing their children scientifically, regardless of their neighbors, and Clay Davis told me he once forced his way to their sleeping porch on a bitter cold day to see if Larry was as cozy taking his nap out there as Frances insisted he was.

Until today I had not met Frances Axtell. Though Don was tall and intense and wrote poetry on the side, Frances seemed small and frail for all the things she could do; and her neutral coloring did not advertise her active mind.

We had supper, and put in a companionable evening, getting to bed early. The Axtells took Larry in with them, and the baby slept on a little mattress on the floor.

Early next morning I got my stuffed frozen turkeys into the oven, and Frances and I chatted companionably as we prepared the other food. Since the kitchen would be too small for so big a dinner, the men put several tables together in the living room upstairs.

Just after noon Slim and Mary Johnson arrived, closely followed by Carter and Phillips. Under her coat Mary wore riding trousers and a gay blouse and the men had new levis and their best wool shirts.

Slim Johnson was droll and easy tongued, with a surprising, highpitched voice, a man never floored by anything. Once on a lonely trail his horse had fallen and broken Slim's arm. He set it himself, right there. After a few days, when he could spare the time to go to town to see a doctor, his arm felt so good he didn't bother.

Mary had taught mountain schools, sometimes "boarding round." When the school was in a feuding district, with only two families represented in the school, moving from one home to the other could be highly exciting. The Johnsons were good managers, ever neighborly, and since they had been married only two years they were still treated as newly-weds.

Dick Carter was frequently at Kirkwood. He was as strong as a horse, and looked at you as directly; and he never whinnied over the improbable or silly. His hair was pale blond and fine, his eyes blue and small, set in a round innocent-looking face.

Till Phillips looked like a mountaineer, brown, and weathered, and on a summer day you rather expected to find him shoeless. He seemed to have an inexhaustible supply of old suit coats, his favorite attire, and when he helped us during lambing I found him full of droll shrewdness and a durable good nature.

While he and Carter put up their horses and Slim's, the Johnsons took their things to the bunkhouse. They would have to share the one room with other sleepers, but a chaste curtain of sheets had been hung down the middle, and Slim and Mary did not mind.

At two o'clock the turkey was borne upstairs to the table, and the other dishes of hot food were placed on either side of it. We adjusted ourselves to the limited seating space, and Len took up his carving tools. The lady guests, one on his right and the other on his left, served the vegetables. While the rest of us chattered my husband gave the children their food first, so they could get started. And now as we began to dine, the radio brought in early reports of football games in the outer world.

We ate slowly and thoroughly. We emptied the serving dishes and I refilled them from the kettles down on the range. There was nothing to make us hurry. And when the wreckage was at last complete, we were ready for pumpkin and mince pie, a slice of each topped with whipped cream, then coffee, nuts and candy. The cooks could now relax.

As the men polished their plates, they smoked and reviewed the state of the nation, about which there was some disparity of opinion. The Axtells in particular were in no doubt about the great figures in the New Deal Administration, and when it came to social and economic theory, Mrs. Axtell could hold her own with anyone.

Mr. Russell, too, could speak with a certain weight. He was very dressy today in his Michigan brother-in-law's trousers, which I had "taken in" for him. Even our current trapper came out of his customary silence, and our other guests responded admirably.

Being deaf, Dick Carter seemed a little left out of things. So when we had cleared the tables and restored the rooms to normal order, I invited him to play checkers with me.

He accepted readily, and I did not mistrust his willingness. As we set up the board his manner was quite innocent, but within three moves I saw that things were not going as I had expected. Dick had maneuvered his pieces indifferently, as if his mind were elsewhere; then suddenly the only moves left to me were expensive ones. A few more plays and the game was Dick's. I wondered how I could have started out so carelessly. We rearranged our men and Dick led, with the same thing happening all over again. I was making every effort to be sharp and Dick was delicately licking his lips.

Patsy and Joe stood at my elbow, watching in disbelief. Mother was being skinned!

I screamed in Dick's ear: "Where did you learn to play checkers?"

"Behind the bars," he grinned. "Lots of time to practice there. That six months I spent, I figgered out all the checker moves and I never forgot 'em."

Though my husband laughed heartily, he did not challenge the champion; in fact no one else cared to try. And as we folded the board, Dick grinned at me, looking very much like a Buddha dressed in a necktie and shirt.

Till Phillips now took out his dollar watch and shook it. He went to the window and looked out into the graying canyon. "Gonna be more snow before morning!" he announced. "Dick," he raised his twangy voice, "we got to be goin'!"

"Oh no!" we begged them. "Stay all night. We've plenty of beds!

But Dick said he had stock that would suffer if he did not go home, and I knew Till preferred his smoke-cured bachelor quarters to anyone else's. The other single men melted away too, and the day was over.

After the chores were done, we had sandwiches and hot chocolate and more pie, then finished the evening with anagrams, which even the Axtells seemed to consider a first-rate game.

Slim and Mary retired to the bunkhouse and Frances and Don to their narrow room. When the living room was safely empty and dark, Patsy took the daybed.

I went outside, just to feel the night. Till's prediction of more snow seemed wrong, for though the air smelled cold, thousands of stars were peering down from the indigo sky. Just over the canyon rim the moon hung in a crescent with the horns up; and the stern dark walls of the canyon were marked by still darker pockets of impenetrable black. Beyond the snowy field I could hear the rustling of the Snake, going down into the night. Except that it was quite cold and Len would tell me I was crazy, I would have gone for a walk up the bar.

In our dimly lighted cubicle, we lay cozy and reviewed our day. It seemed to have gone quite well. My husband yawned, saying, "I feel awfully good about everything. And that dinner was wonderful!"

He hadn't the slightest conception of the planning and labor that had produced the wonderful dinner, but his praise was the final crown of my day.

# 10

I HAD FIRST LAID EYES ON POSY ONE MOTIONLESS NOvember afternoon, when he knocked at the kitchen door with a request so simple that it made me suspicious. He stood there in the vague light looking vague himself, as well as lean and pale.

He said apologetically, "I'm trapping along the river. Would you folks care if I made camp in that old cabin with the roof caved in, at Clark's Fork?"

I looked blank, and he then described the location of the cabin, but it was on beyond Big Bar, which was as far as I had ventured.

"Why do you want to stay there?—it can't be much of a place," I objected.

"I've got a trapline I can reach from that cabin."

"You're welcome to stay in the cabin, of course, but we have a trapper working this range—Max Walker—and we wouldn't want his trapping interfered with."

"I've seen him, but my trapping won't bother him."

The stranger did not hint about staying over night, and since all the men were away, I did not ask him to remain. I guessed him to be about twenty-five, though he appeared even younger. Still twenty-five was an age at which a man ought to know what he was about. So I let him trudge on, to sleep wherever he found a dry crevice when darkness fell.

A few days later he was at my door again, but Len was home this time, and he invited the boy to stay the night. The next morning he came in to breakfast and as I cleared the dishes afterward Posy said: "I saw you cut your finger just now. I'll wash the dishes for you."

"Oh no," I said, feeling I must rebuff him.

He spent most of the day alone in the bunkhouse, but I suppose it was heavenly just to have a dry place with a woodpile handy, and no worry about his next meal.

As Posy came and went I learned more about him. He was actually only eighteen, and he had grown up on the coast, in a fruit-farm area. Later he wintered with an uncle in the Canadian woods, where he learned trapping. Whenever Posy talked about traps and lures, and the mysterious ways of animals, Joe sat motionless, missing not a word; and I confess I too was greatly impressed when Posy told us, for instance, of tracks he had seen that day which indicated a young female coyote had passed a certain point at a rather definite time.

"How do you know that?" I demanded.

And when he explained, his deductions clicked like those of Sherlock Holmes, even though we were some distance from Baker Street; and Holmes, I imagine, had trafficked little with coyotes.

By this time Max had quit the canyon, and Posy was

willing to trap predators on our range in exchange for his board and day wages when there was ranch work he could do. The pelts would be his; he could market them as he pleased. The only government bounty was on cougars, and it sometimes ran as high as fifty dollars; but Posy could hardly expect to get one in the kind of traps he used.

It seemed to be no great hardship for him to forsake his self-directed life and make his home with us. Perhaps he had begun to look on society more affectionately.

At any rate he moved into the bunkhouse, shadowed by Joe whenever school was not holding. As a result the perimeter of garden and pasture began to bristle with the rusty, abandoned traps that accumulate around a ranch; and in these traps we found hens, cats, dogs, and once a female skunk with a family of little ones. Now and then Joe got something more exciting, a coon perhaps, whose skin was good enough to keep. After skinning a usable catch, he dismembered the carcass for the dogs—though they might prove contemptuous—and in this way Joe learned some simple anatomy.

One day he said to me that he thought skunks were not as bad as people said. "They just make this awful smell to save themselves," he explained, "and they keep it in a little sac all by itself."

So much for science.

I liked to have Posy around. There wasn't a thimbleful of meanness in his nature, nor any self-pity. He had not run away from home, he had departed. And he was not imitating anybody or anything. He was just being himself and had simply decided against town life. At an age when most boys prefer the excitement of city living, Posy was filled with a horror of it greater than any fear of hunger, cold or loneliness. His needs were so modest he could carry all his possessions on his back, and his final simplicity was his name. Since he expected no mail, he hardly needed any name but Posy, and we used his real one, which sounded like "bouquet," only to write his checks.

I have seen just one person who could exist in primitive country with even less equipment than Posy. This man was George Lowe, a veteran cougar hunter from the Clearwater valley, who once stayed over night at the ranch. With nothing but a blanket and pack, a rifle and his two hounds, Lowe could drop out of sight into the Idaho wilderness and return weeks later healthy and successful in his quest. He said his staple food was beans, eked out with wild meat. Before starting out each time he boiled the beans and dehydrated them. Then in camp he simply added water to make them palatable. At night he wrapped himself in a blanket and slept by his fire.

I suppose men like Lowe and Posy must first master the art of preventing the unexpected, something it is pretty good to know wherever you live. In any setting devoid of ether and ambulances, accidents are no joke, and survival may turn on their prevention.

We ourselves appreciated this and tried to guard against trouble in every possible way. Nevertheless, that fall we had an unhappy mischance involving a horse.

Len had acquired Cap, a young, short-coupled dapple-gray. When my husband first saw Cap, the asking price was too high for us. Later the horse could be had for less, and we bought him. A strong, sweet-tempered animal, eager for work, Cap was not to replace Eagle—no horse could. But he was to be Len's own particular mount, and being younger, quicker and more docile than Eagle, he was better suited to Len's every-day needs. The children could climb on him safely, but he was not meant to be a barnyard pony when at home. I myself rode him only once, on a steep trail, and the experience was something like going up in an elevator.

We had not owned Cap long when it became necessary for Len to pack supplies from Lucile on the Salmon, a trip too long to make in a day. But this December night, though it was late and the packstring weary, Len had come on home. I was asleep, but when he lighted the lamp it waked me, and I saw by his face that something was wrong.

"Cap's hurt," he said anxiously. "When I crossed the creek at the Carter house he must have jabbed his leg on a broken tree stub. I left him in the field, but as quick as I can unload the mules, I'm going back."

I dressed while he went to wake Mr. Russell in the bunkhouse. We assembled stout cloth, cord, big blanket pins, and a small cloth bag of flour. I mixed a Lysol solution in a jar, and got a tube of surgical gut and a needle, upon which Len looked with doubt. Before we left the house I waked Patsy to tell her where I was going.

"Take me with you," she said anxiously.

"I can't, Patsy. I need you here so that if the boys wake up they won't be frightened. Besides, it'll be cold and dark up the creek."

"Mother, will you come right back?"

"The very minute I can."

"All right," she whispered.

As always, Mr. Russell refused to ride, but he could outwalk any horse, and we pressed ahead rapidly. In the field the lantern showed Cap lying where he had collapsed in a pool of blood on the frozen ground. He turned his wide dark eyes toward us. But he did not move and seemed without hope.

The best thing we could do now was to try to stop the oozing blood. The men examined the torn place high on

Cap's foreleg against his body, and Len sloshed into it the still-warm antiseptic. Next he pushed the bag of flour into and over the big tear and bound it there with strips of cloth and the blanket pins. Cap endured all this submissively. Then gathering up our things and covering the injured horse, we started home.

In the morning, before school, the children hurried up the creek with their father, talking hopefully about Cap. The horse had not moved, but he showed some faint interest when they brought a sheaf of hay from the Carter barn and broke off bits for him to nibble.

He needed a warm shed and warm drinking water, but until he could walk, these were beyond reach. The day would brighten and the temperature rise a few degrees, but night would fall cold and clear again; and though Cap no longer bled, he must be wretched, for he shivered all the time.

The next morning, by patient coaxing, Len got the horse to his feet, but this started the bleeding again, and it was heartbreaking to watch the poor beast's painful progress toward home. Yet to think of him lying on the ground another night was more painful—it was unthinkable.

The trip took an agonizing time, but at last Cap lay sheltered and dry, and we stripped out the disgusting bag of bloody flour. The wound oozed, and Len said it was useless to think of drawing the torn tissues together now. He was overdue in camp, and that evening when I had the Christmas packages ready for the men, he grimly set off on Eagle, expecting to reach Al's camp that night, even though it might be very late.

In the morning Cap seemed a bit better, though he had eaten only a little hay and barely dipped his nose in the warm water we carried to him. I tried putting Epsom salts in one bucket, but he seemed to care neither more nor less for this and jerked reproachfully if I pushed his muzzle into the water.

And now he staggered onto his feet, plainly determined to leave the shed. I let him go out, and he hobbled down through the bright snow-crusty field. He stopped often, then struggled on. Toward evening he had not returned, so I went to hunt for him. He lay in a dry, leafy place under some low brush by the cliff, and would not move. He shook so violently now that I knew there was little hope for him. I fetched a heavy blanket and covered him, and as I left his eyes followed me, but as before, they asked and expected nothing.

In the night it snowed again, and before their breakfast, the children talked pityingly of Cap, out in the cold. But they were convinced that since he had walked around yesterday he would be much better today. The moment breakfast was over they skimmed out across the field to reassure themselves.

Cap's head was stretched out on the ground. They touched him and he did not move at all. They stood about in the snow, not knowing what to do or say; and as they came back to the house I suppose they must have cried a little.

Christmas was but two days away, but even this thought could not lift the depression from their spirits. I tried to keep the conversation on cheerful things, but Joe interrupted me in a stiff voice: "What will Dad do with Cap now?"

"Let's not think about that," I said. "It won't help Cap any."

By the next day Christmas had triumphed somewhat, and toward evening we were further cheered by Len's arrival, bringing a little Christmas tree. He was not surprised about Cap.

"That stub pierced his lung, not just his leg," he said sorrowfully. "Poor old boy!"

In the canyon, compassion toward animals is on the same level as kindness to children, and definitely more tender than compassion for the weakness, loneliness or desolation of any adult.

We trimmed the tree with the cherished baubles of other Christmases, and at bedtime the children hung their stockings near by. They also set out a plate of candy "for Santa Claus," this to convince Steve in case he had begun to have doubts. Naturally, the candy was gone in the morning.

The first lamplight showed a bright sled under the tree for Steve, the same sled that Mr. Russell had found concealed in the granary and was so determined to discuss before everybody. Joe received a fascinating gyroscope top which would pirouette on the edge of a tumbler, and adults could hardly leave it alone. For Patsy there was a toy typewriter that would really print, and that very day she began writing letters. She even copied recipes for me.

The new year crackled in so cold that even the old timers were impressed, and desisted from their tales of the Great Winter—they did not agree on *which* winter it was. River ice tore down so thick and furious it jammed at Kirkwood, and against this bridge fresh ice blocks smashed with an echoing roar. If the current sucked them under instead of flinging them upon the bridge, they grated and battled horribly underneath as if they would rip the barrier apart and send it crashing down the canyon. The thermometer congealed at zero, whereupon Len brought Al and his band from their snow-bound camp, and put the ewes on feed. Each day hay must be sawed from the stack and spread out in the field so that all the ewes would have an equal chance at it.

Ed's camp lay in a warmer and more sheltered draw where the sheep could still get bunchgrass, but if the cold held too long, Ed must be brought down too. The haystacks at Kirkwood, some of them several years old, had been saved for such an emergency.

Neither Al nor Ed would mind sleeping in the bunkhouse and eating my food. Their camps were comfortable enough, but highly standardized as to arrangement and food. A camp consisted of a tent containing a bunk-bed, a stove, and two grubboxes. Usually there were sacks of stock salt, a small tub, bucket and water can, and always a lantern and axe.

Herders' beds were supplied from the ranch, unless the men wished something special, such as a fancy air mattress. Most herders had their own guns; otherwise some sort of firearms would be found for them in the bunkhouse.

Some men got themselves radios or phonographs, and for reading the herders kept a supply of dingy pulps—"shoot'em quicks," Al called them. And the camptender, whoever it was, complained perennially of having to transport bags of old "trash" that herders could not bear to abandon.

Nevertheless the camps were precise in plan, so that when it was time to move, the operation proceeded rapidly. The right number of mules would have been brought; nothing important would be left behind. And when the packstring arrived at the new camp, the tent poles and bed-frame of a year ago might still be at hand.

The tent furnishings were placed in so exact a way that a weary herder, getting in with his sheep after the camptender had done his work and gone, would find everything, down to his sourdough jug, without delay. The stove would be sitting at the left of the door, raised on wooden pegs driven into the ground, their tops protected by empty tins. Beside the stove would be a supply of wood, with pitchsticks or kindling in a separate pile. Across the back of the tent would be the bed, covered with the canvas in which it was packed, with the herder's duffelbag on top for a daytime backrest. On the right would stand the two grubboxes, sometimes raised from the ground. Their tops served as shelves, and their drop-leaf doors became work surfaces.

If the herder liked a wire running along the ridgepole for his towels, dish cloth and spare clothing, it would be in place, and at night his dogs would sleep by the stove or in front of his bunk, ready to dash through the tent flaps if they heard strange sounds among the sheep on their adjacent bedground.

If we were in any doubt about the severity of the cold, we were convinced when the water pipe from the spring froze tight. Then the drain from the sink stopped. The creek froze and for a week we chopped ice to get water for the house and livestock. The only compensation for this additional cold was that we could have icecream, and meanwhile the children went sleighriding on the go-devil, with Kate to pull it.

Around this time, Kenneth Johnson had to get to Lewiston on business, so he left Hazel to spend a week with us, and she brought along *Gone with the Wind*. When the day was done and the others asleep in bed, I sat reading the book in the chilling kitchen, too engrossed to feel the cold, knowing only that this was my one and only chance to read the huge volume through.

No one was ever a more satisfactory guest than Hazel. She knew just how to fill in. She could find a job for herself, and having found it, she never seemed nobly bent on doing it better than I commonly did it. She shared Patsy's room, and they chattered at great length, on a mutual level of understanding that many earnest adults simply cannot find with children.

One evening at suppertime Kenneth rode in. After supper when he found a large jigsaw puzzle half finished on the card table he would not go to bed until the last piece was in place. I understood this weakness because I'm like that myself. Kenneth had a college degree, read political journals and expressed salty views; he had wit and charm, appreciated comfort and good food and without doubt good whiskey. But he *loved* jigsaws!

The thaw had come. The "chinook," a warm wind out of the south, came sighing through the canyon. The plumbing ran again, and life began its spring resurgence. Patsy and Joe broke out with an attack of Indian culture, and their private cubby-holes overflowed with stocks of porcupine quills and feather stems, to be strung in long strings and worn about the neck. They resumed their hunts for arrowheads, and one of them found a beautiful flint scraper, undamaged all these years under plowshare and irrigation shovel. In the boxes of junk by the forge they came on a small rusty axe-head, and got bunkhouse assistance to refit it as a tomahawk.

They visited the little rock pen against the cliff by the tin gate, which some thought a pig pen and others an Indian tomb, but their father forbade them to pull it apart. Instead, he called their attention to the six or eight tepee holes visible along the meadow near the chalk bank. Indians had camped there in long-ago winters. These holes were symmetrically saucered, fifteen to twenty feet across, and when the tepee skins were pegged tight to the *outside* of the saucer rim, rain would run away from rather than into the shelter. The floor being lower in the middle made the tepee warmer, and perhaps the fire in the center drew better for this reason. In the soil of the holes the children found a few arrowheads, mostly imperfect, and layers of river-mussel shells.

For a long time we had had no boat service. Some of our supplies especially tobacco, without which sheepherding cannot go on, were nearly exhausted. However, it was families farthest up, like the Hibbses, who would suffer first. And with the thaw, Esther and Earl Hibbs rode down the river with their baby. They would visit with us until the boat came.

Baby Hibbs did not understand school yet, and Education as an institution had some trouble hanging onto its dignity, but we "managed." When the boat finally came, our guests went down on it, to see the world again.

And I went too. For the first time I went alone, unencumbered by children, free of movement. There was routine business to be seen to, and Len could not leave the ranch. In addition, I had a secret errand to carry out.

In Lewiston I went to every used-furniture store and asked for one certain item, but it seemed to have become obsolete. I merely wanted an old-fashioned parlor organ. But all organs had been converted into tables, desks and whatnots; and salespeople looked at me with pity when I asserted I wanted an organ to play on. Music stores had nothing to offer, and I was about to resign myself to failure when I found one more shop and asked my question for the eighth or tenth time.

"Yes, we have an organ, but it's in a piano box," the nice girl said.

What would prevent them from taking it out of the box? "Could I see it?" I asked, mystified.

She called the manager, and he led me to a back room and pointed. I saw a piano in a rich red wood, with a seven-octave keyboard, and a music rack painted with a quaint bouquet of wild flowers. In their proper place were two piano pedals.

"It's an organ I want," I repeated sadly, "not a piano."

"This *is* an organ, a reed organ. An Estey organ in a piano case. The two pedals work the bellows."

"But does it play!"

"Try it—we've put it in perfect condition."

When the man brought me a chair I sat down breathless. I pumped in a lot of wind, pulled out all the stops and pressed the keys. Bass, treble, every note came true and sweet—and loud. There was simply nothing wrong with this heavenly machine.

Coming back to earth I asked, sighing, "What is the price?"

The man said something that sounded like fifty dollars.

If he had said two hundred I should not have been surprised or insulted. Still I had hoped to pick up a used organ for twenty-five or, at the very most, thirty-five dollars.

"Fifty dollars?" I repeated, relieved that I had never mentioned to Len the idea of buying an organ.

"I said *fifteen* dollars, and we will deliver it for that."

I could have wrapped my arms around the manager. "I want it!" I cried, before he could discover that he had made some fantastic error. "Please deliver it to the Snake River Navigation Dock as soon as you can."

The organ had come! It was being unloaded from the *Chief*. But when it left the boat its troubles had just begun! The go-devil, a sled drawn by whatever horses were available, could not be had at once, and so the Estey rested on the sandbar for a day or two. Then the men loaded it on the sled and drove up through the field. I assumed they would have the intelligence to carry the organ across the creek. But no, they pulled it through the shallow water, satisfied that all of the creek that ran *into* it would run *out* again!

As soon as the organ was placed in the living room, I opened the lid with vast pride and sounded the keys to show off the instrument's dulcet tones. The keys responded—not only the ones I touched, but a lot that I didn't touch! Somewhere inside the organ the wooden parts had swollen with the dampness of the sand and the waters of the creek, and they refused to let go. The confusion was worst in the deep bass, where the moaning was like a foghorn.

For the time I closed the organ in frustration, but when my afternoon's work was done, I brought up the screwdriver and prepared to attack. Everything that would come apart I unscrewed. I found the stuck reeds but I could not quiet them. I tried a makeshift of shifting the keys, both black and white, into different positions and thereby ran into disaster. For though they looked precisely like their brothers in other octaves, there were tiny differences, and I had piled them out with no diagram of their original positions.

Eventually I worked everything back in place, but to stop their complaint I was forced to block off five or six of the lowest bass reeds with strips of adhesive. This kind of cure seemed an insult to the Muses and to Mr. Estey but it would have to do for now. And when I had constructed a piano bench and stained it to imitate the organ, we were ready for music.

We used song books and sheet music and strove for accuracy. Our first attempt was "Home on the Range," what else! And the score showed a verse the children had never heard, with a different tune, too. This new stanza forsook the deer and buffalo and soared to a land of "bright diamond sands" flowing leisurely down to the sea; and there was a graceful white swan gliding along "like a maid in a heavenly dream." The swan seemed a little out of its habitat, but the children were thrilled by the compelling rhythm and the exotic picture, and we were soon ready for daily opening exercises.

MR. RUSSELL OFTEN SAID HE DETESTED SHEEP. NEITHER was he en rapport with horses or mules; and he had never owned or desired a dog. Then somebody dumped on him an orphan puppy, a silky little black ball, with endearing bright eyes. Sourly Mr. Russell allowed it to stay.

Before a week was out, he loved the little thing passionately, and he must have it close to him at every waking moment. No name was good enough for the pup, but it needed none, for it came at Mr. Russell's whistle or call with a rush of affection. One morning Mr. Russell stopped at the house to show me his new treasure. He was hiking to Temperance Creek to do the chores while the Johnsons were outside.

He did not mind going up there, he said. There would be just chickens and cows and turkeys to care for. He admired Hazel's orderly ways, and looked forward to the week he would spend in her house. The walk was nothing, and when the puppy tired, he would carry it.

At first he phoned me nearly every day. The pup was having a big time with the Johnson dogs, and learning fast. Then there came a silence, and the next time Mr. Russell called, he was clearly in some emotional extremity.

"Something's happened," he began in an unnatural voice.

"What is it?" I asked with sympathy.

"I can't tell you, but it's awfully bad."

"Mr. Russell, have you hurt yourself, or are you sick?"

"No, nothing like that."

"Has somebody come, somebody that is trying to make trouble for you?"

"No," he repeated drearily. "It isn't about me."

"Do you want me to send a man up?"

"It wouldn't do any good now."

"Mr. Russell, can't you tell me what's worrying you?" I urged, convinced at last that he was talking about something real.

"No, I can't tell you, so I'd just as well ring off."

"Will you be able to stay until the Johnsons get back?"

"Oh, I won't leave, but I'll never come back here again!"

When Len came home I repeated the conversation.

"The old man isn't sick, you say, and he agreed to stay on, and he doesn't want any of us to come up?"

"That's right."

"Then I'd quit worrying."

A few days later Mr. Russell stopped at our door again. He looked sick, and he carried something in a gunnysack. It was his puppy, dead. It had died in convulsions, right in his arms, Mr. Russell explained tragically. Somebody had come along the river, maybe in the night, and deliberately put out poison for the dog.

We tried to convince him this idea was fantastic, but he shook his head.

"I'm going to bury him in my garden," he said, taking his stick and starting on, "and I'm never going to have another dog—I couldn't bear it!"

In late February Mr. Russell came to stay at Kirkwood a few days while Len would be gone. One bleak afternoon he rushed to the house to tell me that Len's thirty special-purchase ewes, bought three months before and kept at the ranch for closer watching, were beating the gun. They were beginning to lamb.

"What can we do?" I asked desperately. "They can't stand this cold—they must have shelter!"

There was no shed available except the Carter barn, too far away, but Mr. Russell was not one to give up easily. He dragged across the creek enough spare fence panels to surround the big haystack. He lashed them end to end around the stack, then lashed other panels to form a lean-to roof between the encircling fence and the stack. Getting into this tubular shed, he worked hay against the outer wall, then went up on the stack and forked more hay over the roof. When the ewes were pushed inside the shelter, no enemies could get to them; they had the stack both for food and warmth, and the new lambs could not wander off. Besides, no matter how unmaternal a high-bred ewe felt, she could not escape from her baby.

Mr. Russell worked steadily until dark, went over twice in the night, and kept on through the next day, stopping only to snatch a bite to eat. We lost not a ewe, not a lamb, and when Len came he could scarcely believe his eyes.

Mrs. Reynolds rode in on Eagle, and immediately everything around the house was better. We got to bed less exhausted, and our dispositions were sweeter. On Patsy's birthday, however, we were so busy we postponed the event a month, a fairly simple solution if a child knows ahead that this resort may be necessary.

At ten Patsy stood straight and tall and had never spoken to a doctor nor had an inocculation or a "shot." She drove the haywagon when she was needed, and she liked to ride a horse standing erect on its back. She could make cake and raisin-walnut brownbread; and she could sew nicely by hand, though she was rather frightening with the sewing machine. There seemed to be nothing she was afraid of, and she was lonely only if I had to be gone from her, which I rarely was.

However, if I was obliged to be away, she did up all the ironing to make my absence shorter, and when I returned the house was sure to be in order and she and the boys in fresh clothes. This thoughtfulness I shall remember always. I am sure that if your children love you, that is velvet; and any sign of love should be treasured tenderly. Some children can hardly bear their parents, and it isn't surprising. Parents can be tiresome, demanding, jealous and—worst of all—they can sometimes be quite false.

The spring advanced by rapid stages from the first unbelievable over-green green to the burnt beige of shearing time. Everything came to an end, including school. Mrs. Reynolds departed for her home in town, and it was time for trailing.

This June, as always, the ewes and lambs must travel afoot the hundred trouble-infested miles to summer pasture, crossing two rivers, and threading forests, waste land and the lanes that separated cultivated farms. Len laid out the route in exact detail, figuring camping places and water for each night, trying each year to improve on the previous trailing.

Each band had several men with it, and the packer came along with his horses and mules. Sometimes there had to be two packstrings. Toward night the packer went ahead to set up tents and stoves and provide water and wood. In a few places there were stock driveways, but here the grass was already cropped, and the hungry ewes were hard to control.

It was the poorly fenced farms, especially in the hills, that made the most hell, for in spite of the frantic efforts of men and dogs, sheep would invade growing grain, gardens and flower beds, with harrowing results. Some farmers were wholly reasonable about the extent to which they were damaged; but a few opened battle without any preliminaries—and left their fences down to encourage similar damage next year. Women might refuse to close a gate and then impound trespassing sheep and hold them, sometimes with a shotgun cradled in the elbow, while their children streaked to phone the sheriff.

A herder who will joyfully climb a tree containing a cougar will not lay a finger on an angry woman flapping her apron; he will not go an inch beyond wisecracks.

Sometimes Len could buy pasture for the night, and he made friends who not only welcomed him back each year but who would set a meal for the crew besides. Highways could not be entirely avoided, and there the trouble was motorists. Some were overwhelmed when they found they had hurt a sheep; but others drove angrily around a dying lamb and went on.

The weather never stayed wholly fair for three weeks of trailing, and this June it rained unceasingly. The bedrolls got wet and there was no way to dry them out; camps were uncomfortable and cheerless. The gayest herders grew sour slogging though mud day after day.

Whenever they were within reach of a town, Len took the men, by relays, to eat at a cafe; or he brought out hot food and coffee. But towns were a long ways apart.

One sodden afternoon in the middle of the road, Posy said simply: "Len, if you're going to town, throw my gear on. I'm done."

Len protested, but Posy did not yield.

During the long hard spring he had absorbed more punishment than a boy should, but in silence. He had never acquired the art of complaining bitterly when it would do some good. Now he probably saw only one relief, to quit. Of course the day had to be wretched, and there was no one to replace him, anyhow not here in the middle of the road.

Len took him to town, and on the way Posy did not alter his decision.

One spring we tried trucking the sheep to summer range. Another year, with the Forest Service's consent, a route was worked out whereby we missed most of the traveled roads by going through the deep timber, back where civilization was still young. On this route the men encountered some very odd people, all very, very, hospitable. One night they made camp near the cabin of a grizzled old hermit who was spending the winter in his union suit—for him spring had not yet arrived. This mode of dress saved clothes. The old fellow was overjoyed to see other men, and he joined them excitedly at their supper and breakfast talking steadily all the time. This was in exchange for "camping privileges."

That summer's outing was longer for our family than usual, for we visited our various relatives and also hauled to the boat dock in Lewiston the last of our stored books and keepsakes. While away, we went to look over other ranching and grazing outfits, and came home more than satisfied with our own. The children had several weeks of being with other children, and for this I was thankful, for it had been eleven months since they had seen anyone else their own age.

While we were gone, Mrs. Stickney, our neighbor from Johnson Bar, fourteen miles up the river, had canned the Kirkwood blackberries and apricots for both families, and the filled shelves in the cellar were grand to see. It was the usual thing for us to put up a thousand quarts of fruit, vegetables, poultry and meat in the course of a year, but we had never succeeded in drying anything, excepting corn, that entirely pleased us; and we were not skillful in curing meat or fish. My corned venison came out tough, and the "kippered" sturgeon was not good enough to suggest a repeat. Max made venison "jerky" once or twice, and loved to carry brown wrinkly bunches of it in his pocket, to nibble on as he traveled trails between his trap sets; but I had never attempted any jerky, much to the children's disappointment.

As soon as we were unpacked and settled for the winter I went through the supplies of staples, and found these alarmingly low. Moreover, no one could predict when the boat would be able to run. Our best alternative was to pack from Lucile, on the Salmon, and as soon as our new packer could get in, we would lay in grain, hardware and groceries by this route.

It would be weeks before we had fresh meat, but we could manage; there was only one item, laundry soap, about which something must be done at once. Lye is a staple, and we usually had plenty; and for fat, the other ingredient in home-made soap, I searched through every box in the tin storehouse hunting for rancid lard or even drippings that could be strained and clarified. I found all sorts of strange grease in odd camp tins, sometimes mere dabs of it; but when these were added to my hoardings, I had a couple of gallons.

Then, on a chance, I investigated the flat wooden box in the cellar, far back, and came upon a find: ten pounds of old butter—something the packer at shearing time had probably pushed aside without examining. When opened, it smelled not merely unpleasant—it smelled threatening! But it was certainly *fat,* and from some source I must have more fat. So I dumped the ten pounds into the dishpan.

Soap making is one of the simplest and most rewarding of ranch economies. A dairy thermometer is useful but not indispensable. You need a stone crock for the lye, and for the mixing you need graniteware, never aluminum.

The children kept me supplied with wooden paddles at a nickel apiece, to do the stirring; and this must be done slowly, just to the point where the texture of the soap is grainy and honey colored. It is good practice to wear protective glasses of some sort for the job, and to keep cats out of the cooling lye; also to remind children that this is a process during which you can indulge in no foolishness.

When the stirring was done, we covered the soap with a rug and carried it to a warm place for ripening. Then, after a few days, we tested the product and it appeared as fine as any soap we had ever made. Butter *can* be used!

During that year several new names appeared on our payroll. The three older Stickney boys helped us out at times, and Russell Stickney took a band of sheep for a brief period. But Sandy, an eighteen-year-old stranger who walked in one day asking for work, was a new kind of help. He was already repeating phrases of discontent, speaking of labor as if it were an infallible god, and hinting at "revolution." He was infected by an irresponsibility that had begun for the first time to attack farm workers—and farm help had been traditionally honest and dependable. The way we viewed it, this irresponsibility was a by-product of the WPA!

Heretofore our help had not regarded us as an enemy who was to be short-changed on work, stuck for compensation on a counterfeit accident, or discussed with contempt in the bunkhouse. Fortunately Sandy found almost no one to listen to him, and he soon moved on.

"Communism," the word at least, arrived at Kirkwood about this time. Before we met the Axteils, we had read of it now and then; but the Axtells, being Easterners, were familiar with Communism as an idea. If Don and Mr. Russell shared the bunkhouse for a night, I was sure to hear echoes when Don had gone.

"What is this *Communism?*" Mr. Russell demanded of me one day at lunch. "We never had it in Michigan, not in the middle of my forty acres of timber!"

"I know almost nothing about it," I confessed, "but what I've heard worries me."

"It sounds something like Dr. Townsend's Plan," Mr. Russell went on. "Oh, did I tell you I sent my money for his birthday? Well, I did. Everybody's sending him a dollar. Now I don't see as this Communism promises us any cash, leastways not two hundred dollars a month, like Dr. Townsend does. But the Communists are going to get us out of this oppression."

"Oppression? Mr. Russell, do you feel oppressed?"

"Me? Land sakes no! Len Jordan expects you to do your

work, or quit, but he wouldn't oppress nobody!" Mr. Russell laughed extra long, to show he meant no offense.

With Ed Fick, a new herder who had replaced Sam, any vague and passing uneasiness about government was purely academic. Ed was tall and bendable, with a mere halo of blond hair around his shining pate though he was still young and a bachelor. Ed had gone to college, and he liked to eat and argue, one as much as the other, his good nature never flagging.

Earl, another bachelor, a lean, black-haired hill man who had taken over the packing and camp-tending, indulged in no theories at all. He was a crack shot, and during hunting season I was never out of meat. A few weeks after he came, Earl asked Len for some sort of berth for George, his sixteen-year-old brother.

We told him to have George come, so George walked in, spending one night enroute on the top, where he had become lost in the timber. George was as round cheeked and rosy as a new apple, and he had lived first with one family, and then with another, but he was sweet and good. When boat passengers saw the Kirkwood population at the landing and asked him if I was his mother, he blushed. For the present he would help me, wherever I needed him. At the clothes wringer he was strong and quick, and could put through a pair of overalls with a jackknife and a ball of tinfoil as big as an egg in the pocket, and never know the difference.

And before going off to the bunkhouse, George always asked me, "Have you got somep'n else you want me to do?"

It is George I remember when I think of the next new project that filled our lives. For it was George who demolished the final wall that let us into a new existence.

At odd moments Len had begun excavating a space on the north side of the house, toward the creek. Here we had decided to erect a concrete and frame addition that would add a dining alcove, a bathroom, and screened kitchen porch to the ground floor, and a large sleeping porch above. The latter would accommodate the family, and free the two bedrooms for company. The excavating had not yet reached the point where building could begin—it was still in the nuisance stage.

During this pause, there came a lesson for Joe to learn, and the event wove itself somewhat into the fabric of our building problem, the problem of whether to make the effort of going ahead now, or wait another year. From his hoarded allowance Joe had been permitted to buy an air rifle, and on a fall afternoon he had gone exploring, up past the chalk bank, riding Babe bareback and carrying his precious new gun. Babe's bridle had only a snaffle bit.

In the quiet kitchen Len and I talked over the business on which he was planning to leave at once, going out across the divide. I was rather insistent that we must get ahead with the house building immediately on his return, but he had worries of his own and made no promises. That is, he encouraged the project, but he did not guarantee when he would push it further.

He had just risen to go when the door was pushed open and Joe stood there, swaying. He was a shocking sight, his face streaked with blood and dirt, and his shirt bloodstained to the waist. Len and I got him to a chair, and when he had calmed down, we washed his face and felt him over for breaks and bruises.

Joe told us he had started home on Babe, still carrying his gun, but some loose horses along the creek got her excited and he could not hold her with the smooth bit. She tore down the trail in the lead of the other horses and he fell off, landing on his head.

"Why didn't you throw away your gun and get your horse under control?" his father demanded.

"Because I didn't want to break my gun," Joe said.

Len stared at me aghast. How could an eight-year-old reason thus!

The scalp wound seemed small for so much blood, but I snipped the dark hair from around it and flushed out the dirt with disinfectant. Even if the cut had needed stitches, I could not have sewed it. Len, on the other hand, could cut off an arm if it were necessary.

An hour later Joe seemed to feel much better, so Len mounted and started on his way. That night Joe slept exhausted, and it was not until the next morning, while I was attempting a neater trimming around the cut, that I found the real wound, a much bigger one. I soaked the crust of blood out of his hair and poured on more disinfectant. Stiff and sore all over, the child did not protest this treatment, but through the morning every time I passed behind his chair as he toiled at his lessons, there seemed a new odor in addition to the ugly Lysol smell.

We got got through the day, but Joe huddled miserably in the kitchen instead of going out to play. That night I took him in my bed, and presently he appeared to sleep. But I had barely closed my own eyes when he struggled up and began clawing the air and uttering senseless words. It took a long time to calm him, and after that my own fears were too great to sleep with.

George had gone to help with some corral building up the river. On leaving, Len had not been sure where he would be himself for the next few days, so I did not know where to call him. I could not be sure of anyone's coming along. It was true there was a horse that could probably be caught, but how long did I dare wait before making up my mind to take Joe out, leaving Patsy and Steve behind? Twenty times before dawn I woke with a terrified start. Sometimes Joe was mumbling.

"I'm betraying him! Maybe it's already too late!" I told myself in panic.

In the morning I felt hardly better than Joe, but I knew I must show no sign of alarm. Joe ate little breakfast, and afterward he went doggedly at his lessons, too pale and dull minded to accomplish much. Again he spent the afternoon inside.

Each day that week was like the one before, and always the pervading odor of antiseptic.

Finally one afternoon the phone rang. Cheerfully and clear my husband's voice came in. "Hello, Grace! How are you all? I'll bet you'd never guess where I am—right up at Temperance Creek!"

Why is he at Temperance Creek? I wondered heavily.

His business had proved more complicated than he expected, Len said, and an interesting new lead had developed. It took him around into Oregon, where he had had a visit with his folks. And meeting Hazel Johnson and Anna Maxwell, who had been in Enterprise for the summer, he had been glad to accept a ride to the river on one of their horses. It had been a pleasant trip.

I was too worn and dull to respond to his cheerfulness.

"I'll stay here tonight and come down tomorrow some time," he went on pleasurably. "I'll see you then, honey."

I did not answer. There were no adequate words.

"Are you still there?" he asked, moving the hook up and down. "What's the matter?"

"Nothing."

"I'd come on home this evening, but it's a bother for Kenneth to put me across now, and everybody's tired. I'll just visit while I'm here, and get home tomorrow. Maybe Kenneth'll bring me down himself!"

Carefully I replaced the receiver.

In a few moments the phone rang again.

"Hello," I said.

"I'll make it down tonight," my husband said stiffly.

Len barely drew his breath at home before announcing he must get off to camp. Joe was getting along fine, he thought; there was nothing for me to be worrying about.

During the next week it rained continuously. The excavation outside the kitchen door became a mudhole that must be scrambled through each time I passed, and I saw that it would remain like that for indefinite weeks. Farm work, packing, camp-tending and work with the bucks would rate unlimited attention; the house was due for little or none. The situation was coming out in sharp clarity.

One evening Earl and Len rode in from camp with their problems all nicely in hand. They looked relaxed; they ate a big, hearty supper. That night Len slept the sleep of the weary and the just; he rose to a pancake breakfast, and then sat smoking and reflecting, while the children and I worked against the clock to be ready for school at eight-thirty.

The morning had broken bright and crisp. A faint breeze ruffled the surface of the excavation pools. Without doubt, it was going to be a lovely day. Len went to the phone and rang Kenneth. "I've got a clear day at last," he said. "If you're going to be at home, why don't I ride up for a good talk with you?"

The answer must have been pleasing, for my husband replaced the receiver with an air of anticipation and self-approval.

"That's fine," I said, rather loudly. "If you're going to be away it will give me a full day for packing. I can see we aren't going to get any building done this fall, so I think it will be best if I take the children out to town and put them in school. We can just about catch the next boat."

Len stared as if he doubted his own hearing. His look gradually became that unspoken question most maddening to an aggrieved woman: "Is she sick or something?"

In the silence I went upstairs. I did the beds. I did the living room. I put away things. It could not have been forty-five minutes later when I came down, but in that time the mudhole outside my door had become a ferment. Men, lumber, saw-horses, a wheelbarrow, picks and shovels were in motion, with children interspersed. A saw began to squeal. A hammer pounded. Looking out discreetly I saw Mr. Russell arrive, tying on his carpenter apron as he came.

I did not open the door and exclaim.

The children rushed in, excited, and we began school, but they could hardly keep their minds on their work, and the moment they were free they rushed out again to see what was happening now.

Lunch was a mere pause. The tools scarcely cooled. I now went out to look, and already the forms for concrete walls were taking shape.

It went on that way all day, with no delay whatever, for the materials required had all been laid in—cement, screening, lumber, shingles, window-sash, paint. By nightfall it looked as if a week's work had been accomplished, and there was much laughter and self-esteem all around.

On the next boat Len ordered not only the hot-water tank, the complicated piping, sewer traps, soil pipe, drain tile, and so forth, but as another sign of the triumph of modernism in our canyon, a certain snowy object that has been called by many names, not all of them stately. To the Continental, I understand, it is a commode; to plumbers, a stool. We being neither Continental nor plumbers merely admired it unashamed as its wrappings fell away. For the moment, we placed it where neither time nor rust was likely to corrupt it—in the living room.

Compared to contract work, where delay can invoke painful penalties, our operation moved at a snail's pace; yet by canyon time, which is fairly eternal, it went at admirable speed. Every man who rode along and had spare time and the slightest skill, was given a shovel or hammer, and put on the payroll. I was expected only to keep meals cooking and to go out and give a periodic okay.

In a few days the four-foot concrete walls were done, and those of the alcove were topped by a bank of window openings on two sides, all of which was no great feat for the jack-of-all-trades that every remote rancher becomes. The real brain-twister ahead was the construction of a concrete bathtub and washbasin, and hooking these to our water supply on one end and to the concrete septic tank with scientific baffle on the other end.

Along the route, there would be the hot-water tank heated by coils in the range. The water hook-up through tank and coils was to be no picnic either, so Celia Titus warned Len by phone when she heard what we were doing. Celia reported that when they first hooked up the Titus tank the water ran the *wrong* direction and might well have blown them all through the window and into the river!

Further complicating the bathtub riddle was the fact that to conserve space and at the same time put water intakes and outlets for the tub and basin close together, Len proposed to extend the tub *through* the bathroom wall, where it would become the hollow pedestal of the washbasin on the porch! The only possible objection to this clever arrangement was absurd: simply that a bather could not stand upright in the extreme intake end of the tub. But the children found this an extra advantage—it made a wonderful place for hiding!

Designing the tub forms took many an evening with graph paper. Sketches must be made to scale for the four sides, others for top and bottom, and the labor was doubled by the fact that there must be both inner and outer forms.

The outer form was to be made of wood, the inner form tin on wood braces, and the tin was to be filled with sand to hold it in place during the drying. After extensive trial and error the forms were worked out, then concrete was mixed in special proportions, with special gravel and sand.

Now the mixture was poured and tamped, poured and tamped, with jealous care, without stopping, for as long as it took. There was an anxious wait while the concrete hardened. When the inner form was lifted out, and rather ceremoniously at that, we beheld a mud-colored rather gritty-looking stone box, and the idea of getting into it naked was disturbing, but this was a silly thought for there was a great deal yet to be done. The broad rim would be rounded gently, the edges beveled, and the inside corners coved. Then there would be resetting, re-inspection, more building up and scraping off, more rounding and coving.

All this was finally done, and at long last the tub was as good as one could hope to make it. The glaze coat of cement was now washed on, and after another extended spell of drying and ripening, we put on coats of primer and ultimately the last touch, white enamel. One coat of this followed another until the surface felt like satin—that is, almost like satin.

There was no way we could hurry these processes, and for many a Saturday night to come we would bathe in the washtub, screened from sight, close to the pulsing hot breast of the Monarch.

Shaping the washbasin presented one new problem, though in comparison to others it seemed hardly more than a trifle. "What does a ranch household contain," my husband pondered, "that is shaped like the inside of a washbasin? A wooden chopping bowl, of course. Build up the bowl with a slightly flared collar and you have it!"

I handed over my chopping bowl.

All the intricate pouring and finishing processes applied to the bathtub were applied as well to the washbasin, and when the basin was done it had everything, including a substantial, hand-made look.

Creation is making something from nothing; and creation is as bad for tying up a man's day- and night-time thoughts as the drug habit. Yet it is soul-satisfying, and for the weeks that we were involved in the carpentering and plumbing arts, we had never been happier.

To be sure there is one obvious difference between producing a masterpiece in painting or music and a masterpiece in concrete: if the creator of a picture or a symphony is disappointed in his results, he can toss his creation out the window. But try tossing away a concrete bathtub!

Long before our house-building was done Earl and George had assumed all the packing and farm work; but Mr. Russell stayed on as assistant carpenter. With the walls of the first floor done, the frame for the second story was quickly finished and the gable was built on the ground and swung into place by pulley. When it was anchored and braced, the house looked twice its former size. Soon the men had everything enclosed against the weather, which had been quite gracious until now. When the screening of the sleeping porch was finished and the windows and doors hung, only two major tasks remained: to tear down the concrete wall between the old kitchen and the alcove, and to lay a new concrete floor throughout.

To George was assigned the task of razing the wall. He attacked the seven-inch barrier with hammer and spike, pecking away by the hour whenever school was not keeping. Dust soon whitened everything; we breathed it, we ate it. As the wall crumbled, George became coated himself, more thickly each day, but he loved the importance of his office as chief destroyer. And as each day the kitchen grew lighter and airier, I felt like the chambered nautilus, getting more stately mansions added to my soul.

Since we could not vacate the kitchen, the floor had to be laid in sections, with plank cat-walks over the travel lanes. Staying on these walks took balance, but it was amusing and so were the immense prints that George's feet made in the soft concrete one morning when he burst in the door for breakfast. Without complaint, the master mason soon smoothed them out, at the same time eradicating some kitten prints on the back porch.

Now it was my turn to help. I painted the inside window frames and doors white, and to all wall and ceiling surfaces I applied my ivory chalk-bank kalsomine. In the bathroom I pasted black and white tile cloth for a wainscot, and made a supply shelf above the casement window. Fortunately water pipes were at just the right height to serve as towel rods. Though the back wall stayed warm from the range, we silver-painted an old kerosene heater for supplementary warmth. I cut down a fruit crate to fit the only space left for a clothes hamper, and with a hinged lid and a coat of enamel, it looked quite adequate.

As insurance against future disaster, my plumber left an opening in the concrete bathroom floor to permit access to the waste pipe. The opening was the precise size of a stovelid, and Len closed it with just that. The lid lay flush with the floor, so that the sliding door would pass it; and it could be removed with the regular stovelid lifter.

The bunks on the sleeping porch were nearly done now, and the children could hardly wait. It would be almost as good as "sleeping under the stars," one of their father's favorite allusions, and a mode of slumber they seized whenever possible. French doors gave access to the porch through the living room, and when I had curtained these and the new windows in kitchen and bath, we seemed to have completed our assignment.

Meanwhile the golden fall had blazed and died, bucking season had passed, and we were approaching the shortest day of the year. On the night of December twenty-first, which was starry and sharp, the beds on the porch were pronounced ready for the family, and we took possession with some eclat. Joe and Steve drew the lower bunks, Patsy the upper one with a little ladder. Snug in our wool covers, we could plainly hear the call of the creek under its icy fringe, and the distant rush of the Snake was louder now. These sounds only added to our sense of security.

It was on an afternoon two weeks later, that the bathroom was finally finished.

"The tub's ready to turn on," Len stated. "All set to go!"

"Who's going to take the first bath?" the children demanded. They were not interested in the fact that history was about to be made, that someone bearing a towel in one hand and a bar of soap in the other would, in a few minutes, be ushering in the Era of Concrete—all they wanted was to turn on the water and see the tub fill, then leap in!

My husband patted my shoulder. "It'll be Mom. She gets the first bath. She's the bathingest person in the family, and besides, she deserves it! Come on, Mom!"

I tried to respond graciously, but it was past time to start supper. So I said, "I can't take a bath now. But you could. *You* take the first one, Len."

He needed no coaxing. He was dying to try his creation.

The boys were at his heels. The little door closed the three in, and within a few minutes, sounds of ecstasy were reaching me through the stone wall. Then the boys came running to ask, "Can we take a bath too?"

I felt the tank. "Yes, you can each get a bath if you hurry."

At bedtime Patsy and I took a formal turn each. Thus an event new in the canyon and unlikely to be repeated was notched in the annals of the Snake.

On the cold porch I listened to Steve's prayer: ". . . and make me a good boy. Mother, why didn't Dad *buy* a bathtub and a washbasin? They wouldn't be *nicer,* but they would be quicker."

"Because he was short on space. A 'store' washbasin can't be set on the end of a 'store' bathtub."

"Oh!" he said sleepily. "Amen."

# 12

THIS WAS THE YEAR DELL BECAME OUR MAN. EARLIER we had observed him coming and going as he fished for sturgeon along the river. To market his catch, he had to depend on the boat, and it in turn depended on the weather and the stage of the river. A six- or eight-foot sturgeon waiting to be butchered could be left tied to the willows like a horse hitched to a post, but not for very long; and sometimes when the boat was delayed Dell had to release his fish.

Sturgeon are ugly. They look like sharks, with their heads taking up a large part of their total length, their mouths set far under their snouts and their jaws overhung with creepy whiskers of flesh. Down their backs they exhibit spiny dorsal plates. A few years earlier sturgeons that would "fill a wagon bed" were often reported caught in the Snake, and I saw one that thirty people dined on for three days. But by this time a seven- or eight-footer seemed very satisfactory.

Once when the boat was delayed, Dell tried starting down the river with several sturgeon hitched abreast to a raft. It was exciting enough in the rapids, but when the sturgeon tired of the game and took to the brown boils at the side, Dell had to quit the raft in a hurry.

Not tall to start with, Dell seemed to grow shorter and stronger with each season, as if concentrating his inner forces for whatever lay ahead. In his time he had farmed, packed, herded sheep, and done nearly everything that is ever done on a sheep ranch. His children lived with their mother, and his home was wherever he found work, but he was very mindful of the children's welfare and so happy if they wrote to him.

He was a good shot, loved horses and got on well with them; he was slow, thorough, and afraid of nothing and no one. Though he missed his own children, he found pleasure in other people's, without inviting them to encroach. If he had worries or was sometimes drenched in loneliness, the only evidence was the affection he showered on Gyp, his little black dog.

The first time he was due for a layoff, Dell brought in a blue serge suit and asked Patsy to press it. She strove to do this nicely and while she was about it, reinforced buttons and repaired a rip. When Dell returned from his leave he brought her a present, and after that he began remembering all three of the children's birthdays.

With Dell to fill in wherever a special lift was needed, our spring tensions seemed easier, and Len and I found time to think about a project that concerned Patsy. It would cost a bit, but our rigidly maintained budget had taken care of the second payment on the ranch before it was due, and we were feeling less cramped.

Patsy was eleven, old enough to profit from two weeks

at a summer girls' camp on Coeur d'Alene Lake, far away in the timbered northern part of the state, and we decided that an experience of this kind should not be regarded as a luxury.

Following a prescribed list, Patsy and I made some of the clothing needed and sent away for the rest. When the last item was checked off and laid in her travel bag, we felt quite thrilled. Meanwhile there was her school work to finish.

Her last assignment in English was a three-lesson theme, an ambitious effort designed as a test for the year's work. She was allowed to choose her own topic, and after lengthy discussion we decided that it would be fun to write about the Indians that had once hunted on Kirkwood Bar, used the tepee holes up the creek, and lost their arrowheads here and there.

By this time, the children had collected quite a box of arrow- and spear-heads, from tiny ones intended for birds to big ones for deer and elk. Some were of flint and obsidian, some of stone we could not identify. A few were still perfect. But it was at the natural creek crossing that the children picked up most of the incomplete or imperfect heads, and Len thought this might be the spot where the squaws, who had the responsibility of shaping the heads, had done their patient work.

All an Indian needed for this nearly forgotten art was a fire to heat the stone, and a straw with which to drop water on the spot where the chip must come out. "Conchoidal" cleavage was necessary if a thin, cutting edge was to be achieved, and this cleavage is given to flint and obsidian in particular. But these were not found along the river, and it seemed that the Indians must have brought their material here to shape it, perhaps during their hunts.

According to Lewis and Clark and other explorers, the Indians had belonged to the tribe now known as Nez Perce. By good fortune we owned the diary of Captain Bonneville, edited by Washington Irving, which covered the Bonneville Expedition of 1832 and described our very own section of the Snake River. The captain dwelt on the kindly nature and impressive physique of these Indians, and we found several stirring paragraphs that could be quoted in entirety.

So Patsy used this material and drew on all the inference we could make concerning the life of the vanished Nez Perces on our bar and creek. Her father checked this section of her paper sternly, to eliminate any fancy, ill-founded generalizations. In the final copy, Patsy made small colored drawings of both Indian weapons and utensils, then consigned her effort to the mail.

When the report came back from Baltimore, she had won commendation and a gold star, and the star brought her a dollar from her father. In addition she had learned that historical material may be found in many places, even in a shabby old book, and that her faraway teachers considered it no grave misfortune to be growing up in a canyon.

With her year's work done, Patsy could relax; and having finished early, she would be allowed to go to shearing camp. The trip would be justified because she could help Mrs. Reynolds. For as it turned out, the Stickneys brought down their sheep to shear with ours, and there were more men to feed and more people to enjoy than usual.

Just before shearing, and due to government price-fixing, wool plummeted in price. Moreover we got word that we might have trouble disposing of our wool unless it was certified as shorn by a union crew. A sheep-shearer's union in the depths of Snake Canyon was patently absurd, but the 1938 path of the American livestock man, a normally independent and rugged creature, was certainly not strewn with government roses.

The year as a whole, however, had been good, and we had bought a new gas washing machine *minus* a gas engine, which we secured separately. The reason for a separate engine was this: it could be taken to camp and used for tagging (removing the ewes' untidy or blinding tags of wool). But whenever the engine was away it picked up bad habits, and I would be unable then to start it until some gas-minded man happened along. Still, when it was at home, it could be used to charge batteries for the radio and it also made juice to run four small electric lights which Len installed in the house, respectively at the table, over the stove, in the cellar, and in the living room.

In a town house the six-volt light would have been considered an insult to human eyesight. No one would be physically able to read by it. But after you have mended, cooked and watched the sick by kerosene light, six-volt illumination is dazzling.

Our cellar light was a great blessing, and to make sure it was not left wastefully burning when not in use, my husband put a switch outside the door. This switch had once ennobled some dead automobile panel, but our little blob of light responded impartially to its *Full* or *Dim,* and when it said *Off* it meant off.

The living-room light, too, was modern in operation. By the stairs there hung a little red handle from a pancake turner, and if you wished to go up after dark, you tripped this handle, saying in effect, "Let there be light." And instantly there was.

Joe and Steve had finished their year's lessons, the wool was shipped and off our minds, and summer was peering in over the canyon rim. Dell started the sheep to summer range while Len began haying.

Just at this time a sudden change occurred in the boat service. A stranger to us, Kyle McGrady, had bid successfully on the mail contract, without which Brewrink and McFarland did not care to handle freight and passengers on the up-river run from Lewiston. But neither did they wish to sell the reliable old *Chief Joseph.* So around the first of June, up came a new boatman-mailman, with a new arrow-thin craft.

McGrady was a brown, nervous, resolute-appearing man, young enough and strong enough for the river; he seemed forever on the verge of a stirring adventure and frequently proved to be. By early summer the water was dropping so fast he expected to make only one more passenger run, after which he would use an outboard motor on a sea-sled and, until high water in the fall, would carry nothing but the mail.

Patsy's camp date was imminent, and I was to take her to the lake. Since Len could not spare the time to get us to a bus on the highway, it was clear we must go out with the new boatman on his last passenger trip.

The entire household came down to see us embark. The McGrady boat was so new the engines had not yet been housed, and the passenger cabin amidships was not much more than an overgrown box. However, Patsy and I seated ourselves comfortably in its shelter, and relaxed to the delightful bobbing of the eddy. The air was still crisp, and a breeze played on the ripples close to shore. McGrady had an assistant, and as they were both experienced on the lower river, Len felt no misgivings about our going down with them.

Later in the day the canyon would swelter in the heat, but now Patsy wore her new blue jersey coat with the red silk lining to keep it from wrinkling; and she carried a very precious item in blue plastic that, as a traveler to far places, she would surely require. It was a little handbag, her first.

As the engines sprang to life we waved goodbye to Kirkwood. Soon we were skimming excitedly down the reaches of shadowed water, through lesser rapids, in and out between the twisting walls, perhaps no faster than one rode in the *Chief Joseph,* but with a greater sense of aerial flight.

As we flashed past Mr. Russell's estate, he waved at us. The old house at Kirby Bar was there for a few moments, then hidden behind a headland. At Circle-C and Pittsburg we paused for mail, then flew on. We swooped past the mouth of Summers Creek, and shot into the rapids below, but after that we lost track of distances because there were no more ranches, only towering bastions. The sun had topped the wall, and tired from our early rising hour, we felt drowsy—drowsy and at peace in our warm little cabin.

Then, without warning, everything changed on the treacherous Snake. Swept across a glassy pool, we went diving down a cascade of gray-green water with vicious rocks sticking out and unseen rocks ripping at the bottom of the boat. McGrady held the course and got us through and down into deeper water, but here we tossed in a foaming welter then plunged down another steep chute. As we hit bottom a wall of spray broke in over the engines.

Instantly the boat ceased to plunge. Without power it tossed at the mercy of the rapids. The two men at the engines shouted to each other, McGrady clinging to the wheel and the other man dragging in frenzy at the starter. But our engines were dead, we were out of control and we were centered on a perpendicular cliff that rose sheerly from the mad current.

McGrady struggled with the rudder, but the power of the Snake was too much for his long, thin craft. We were going to strike the cliff, and when we did, I expected the boat to be hurled back into the pouring cascades and submerged. Some hidden ledge might catch and hold us a moment, but I saw no other hope.

"Patsy," I said as calmly as I could, "we may hit those rocks. If we do, you and I must get on the roof. That will put us up higher. Drop everything when I tell you, and start climbing out!"

"Mother," she cried tensely, "do I have to leave my handbag?"

"Yes! Watch closely now. I'll tell you when!"

But as we tossed nearer and nearer the cliff, McGrady's desperate assistant got life into one of the shorted engines. With this much power McGrady shot us back into the channel and we tore past the waiting cliff. I could not hear what the men were shouting, and even under our canopy we were taking spray, but the boat bumped safely down a few more rocky staircases, then fell into fairly quiet water. Finally we pulled into a sloping shore bordered by a sandbank.

No one moved or spoke for a moment.

Then McGrady stopped the one engine, and I watched him perform a remarkable feat. Mooring the boat to a thorn tree, he got down in the water in his clothes and reached under the hull. He hammered and wrenched until he had loosened the propeller shaft, which was nearly as long as the boat itself. He drew it out completely, and with the help of his man, tugged it on shore. When he had found a rock suitable for an anvil, he hammered out of the shaft the kinks that the rocks had put in it.

He did all this with no lengthy sitting and pondering, without worrying over whether it had ever been done before.

When he had restored the shaft we were ready to proceed with both engines. And we had lost merely an hour from our schedule. Patsy and I ate our sandwiches and settled for a pleasant ride, though with little hope of a breeze.

The remainder of the trip to Lewiston and the following day to the lake were uneventful. In Coeur d'Alene we stayed at a hotel, a rare experience for Patsy; and the next afternoon we crossed the lovely forest-fringed lake on a boat filled with twenty other unknown girls. For the most part they had come from an area within an hour of the lake and were not entire strangers to each other. Nevertheless a few had wept at parting from their mothers.

I was shown a clean camp that hummed with activity, and met the women in charge. When we had made Patsy's bed and visited with her new tent-mates, it was time for me to leave. Patsy went with me to the dock, clinging to my hand, and at the very last moment she stared at me with a stricken look.

"Here, here!" cried one of the flat-soled counselors, a hearty young woman from Iowa. "What's the matter! Crying isn't allowed!"

I smiled; and though her eyes burned, Patsy managed an answering smile. So I turned her over to the good Iowan and got into the launch quickly—before I too should be reproved.

From the hotel in Coeur d'Alene where we had slept I wrote Patsy a note, telling her explicitly what she should do in case I was late when I returned for her in two weeks. She was to come from the boat to this same hotel and wait. It was perhaps a hundred and fifty yards from the dock and as visible from the dock as her right hand. She would only need to tell the clerk that she had been attending the camp and was waiting for her parents. Then he would know how to aid her if I was more than an hour or so late, which of course I did not expect to be.

Len wound up the haying with speed and took the boys out to Grangeville with him, then on to camp. Later the three joined me in Grangeville and at the end of Patsy's two weeks we all started north one morning to get our girl.

We parked at the dock, and when the first boatload of Patsy's contingent arrived, I was close at hand. I watched each girl come off, and Patsy was not among them. Another launch came, and I was with the parents that greeted it. Patsy was still missing. Presently the third and last boat came. Among the very last passengers off was a tense child in camp uniform whose eyes searched the chattering groups of girls camp-bound and girls home-bound milling about with their parents.

Patsy failed to find me in the crowd. No one had come for her! I called her name, but she did not hear. She went and stood by her bedroll and bag.

When I touched her arm she looked at me dazed. We walked in silence to the car, but even after her things were loaded and we were off, she said nothing, barely answering our questions. For the next twenty-four hours she was too ill to eat, and her father gazed at her in anxious gloom.

But suddenly she was better, and with her returning gaiety, the positive gains of her two weeks in a new world came into focus. She had made several warm friendships among girls and counselors; she had learned to swim, to do hand crafts, to be one of a team presenting stunts and games; and above all, she had learned to meet unexpected situations.

It was the second day that she said, "Did I tell you I had to make a speech?"

"Where, and what was it about?" her father asked gently, trying to sound enthusiastic.

"Over in Coeur d'Alene at the Kiwanis dinner," Patsy explained. "They asked me because I was the girl that had come the farthest distance. It was a very nice dinner, and they had it in a big room, with lots of men. The counselor went with us, and she showed me how to write some notes for my speech, but I forgot to look at them."

"Kiwanis!" Len muttered, looking at his first-born with considerable respect.

# 13

WE WERE RESOLVED TO FIND A WOMAN FOR YEAR-round help. If we could secure a married couple, that would be still better, though our house was clearly too small for a couple with children. Len's management had increased our wool and mutton returns, but at the same time his new projects for bettering our physical plant, improving our crops and trying out new range grasses tended to keep our household large. School was constantly demanding more of my time. All considered, help in the kitchen had become a necessity.

During the time we were out, that summer, I made several visits to the nearest government employment agency, ran down the few hopeful leads, and discovered for myself the new thinking among some of the employed. Help tended now to be the bargainer. It took for granted the highest prevailing wage, was inclined to dictate conditions, and claimed the right to quit without warning. Employees were safe in their position, for the government virtually guaranteed employment, and it also provided the unemployed with various "commodities." If a government agency sent you a worker and if you fired him, regardless of your *reason* for discharging the man the agency might refuse to send you another. The government had become our competitor.

Though I offered standard wages, there was not a single taker. People did not care to go where movies and dances were beyond reach; or they were afraid of getting sick away from a doctor; or they didn't think they'd like living in a canyon.

The only half-eager prospect was an ill-nourished husband and an over-nourished wife. They had come from the south in a decrepit car teeming with children under and over school age. We passed them up and I went on inquiring and writing.

At last I heard of Florence, in a little Washington town. She had a husband and children, the youngest a little girl of five, but Florence's mother could look after the family, and Florence wanted to earn some money. I met her at a store and we talked. She said she was tired of the government-run sewing room, where material was free and she could make clothes for herself and the children. She said the lady boss of the sewing room was snoopy. If Florence was also tired of matrimony, that, I felt, was none of my affair.

Florence was black-eyed and buxom, calm and ignorant. But she liked to cook—her lard cake was especially good, she said. Little Clarice, who would have to accompany her, was either shy or sullen, it was hard to tell which.

With misgivings, but determined not to give up, I arranged for Florence to come to the ranch by boat. If she was tired when she arrived, or dismayed by the river, she did not show it. She seemed happy just to survey a cupboard full of supplies, and to have a room for herself and Clarice.

The first morning, Florence rose as soon as she heard anyone stirring, and from then until bedtime she worked with scarcely a pause, Clarice bobbing in her wake like a little wet shingle. The child made no sound and was hardly perceptible until placed at the dinner table. There she sat hanging her head and seemed in danger of starving until the chicken plate came along, when with shocking intensity she seized a drumstick in one hand and a thigh in the other. Her mother removed the second piece from her grasp, but Clarice hooked it again as it went by on the next round. For dessert she consumed a large piece of warm mince pie, rapidly, and whispered to her mother for more.

Florence turned doubtfully to me.

"Of course," I said, hiding my astonishment. "There's another pie!" Clarice must be filled up; that was elementary.

It turned out that Florence could barely read, and when you gave her a recipe to follow, you were in for a surprise. For example she thought that chili con carne was chili with a can of corn.

Florence was afraid of the gas engine, so I did the washing. When she admitted being suspicious of the gas iron too, I gave her the old-fashioned stove irons, and with these she toiled by the hour, the perspiration standing on her broad, dark face.

The first afternoon that I suggested a two-hour rest, since there was nothing urgent to be done, she stared. "I ain't tired," she protested in a bothered way, "and I wouldn't know nothin' to do anyhow."

"Well, you could look at a magazine or go for a walk."

"I'd juz soon set and talk to you," she said lonesomely. "I been tryin' to 'magine what they're doin' at home, them Kaisers and Dawsons next door. An' my niece an' her family. Probably all talkin' about *me*."

"Then why don't you write them a letter, Florence?"

"It's too hard work. But I'll write 'em one when I send 'em my check. *He'll* pay me in a check, won't he?"

Color immediately began to show in Clarice's pasty cheeks, and Florence put on more weight. She worked hard, always, but it was clear she could not learn much. I explained many things, over and over, and she would say, "Looks like I ain't been doin' somep'n igzactly right!" Occasionally I asked her to re-do the whole ironing, but she only smiled as she sprinkled the pieces again.

Clarice seemed to own but one change of clothes, which soon fell apart. It was lucky that we had a supply of small out-grown overalls. Florence also seemed to have but two dresses, new when she arrived, and as she put on more flesh, their seams parted and their buttons flew. Florence repaired them with safety pins.

One afternoon I was spading under the grape arbor and found where someone had dug a recent hole. In it were buried tobacco tins of a kind none of our men carried. Poor Florence, she could not even enjoy her one vice in sociable comfort. What was she going to do when her papers and tobacco ran out—maybe they were gone already!

At the first opportunity I slipped some packages of Camels under her pillow, and they were not returned to me.

One Saturday the boat brought Florence a gummy letter, and all day long she was silent and remote. That evening when we were alone she reported that everything at home was okay, and they had sure needed her check. Jim (her husband) would like to come to Kirkwood for a visit, as he was "feelin' porely and not workin'."

She studied my face as she said this. "Just to see what everything here looks like," she added artfully. "Jim, he can't understand how a place is so steep. He says he'd come fer a visit, so if you would need him to work in the spring he'd know if he'd want to hire."

"No, Florence," I said firmly, "we're too busy now for visitors."

"Okay," she chirped, smiling broadly. This meant, "I just mentioned it—I sure don't want that man here neither—underfoot!"

A few days later a pleasant stranger, stopping for dinner, said to my husband: "You have four children, I see. I heard you had only three."

I saw a startled look in my husband's eyes, and like automatons we all turned to Clarice. She had chosen this moment to begin on her pie, and much of it was on her face. Florence winked confidentially at me as she took up the edge of the tablecloth to clear Clarice of her sin—Florence never used her napkin; it made too much washing.

"Clarice!" Florence scolded fondly. "Now you let that pie alone! Tain't time for pie. You eat more meat!"

Florence sought to move the pie plate away, but Clarice seized it in her skinny little hands and bleated, "No! No! I want pie!"

Clarice hung her head; but the stranger was still staring.

That night I faced the facts. Florence was striving with all the brains and the strength she had, but they were not enough. Her help was not equal to the embarrassment she brought. But her family needed the money she was earning, and I debated painfully where to dráw the line between charity and hard common sense.

While I waited for the right moment, the household acquired a new member. This was Bob, small, middle-aged, spotless, a bachelor who did not smoke or drink, and wanted no coffee. Also, he explained, he had a fussy stomach, and could eat nothing made with cocoa or chocolate, whereupon Florence was done with him. We could never have a chocolate cake now, she said when we were alone. This man was not to be trusted! He'd prove to be no good—she could tell!

When I told her that Bob was to have sheets on his bed, because he was used to sheets and preferred them, she gaped. And later finding his neat broadcloth pajamas in the wash, she held them up giggling. When I said they were to be ironed, she appeared about to gag.

On the following Sunday morning I went to the garden to dig parsnips. This vegetable achieves its best flavor when it has been frozen a bit, and since the digging would be somewhat hard, I knew I should have no offers of help to interrupt my thinking. When I returned to the house, my mind was made up, but to break the news to Florence, who sang of unrequited love as she prepared dinner, took all the resolution I could summon.

"Florence," I said abruptly, taking my stand a few feet from her, "I want to talk to you. I'm going to have to let you go. My plans have changed. If you want to go out on the next boat, I'll pay your fare and give you a check for the extra two weeks of the month."

As Florence turned to me I saw her black eyes filling up with tears. They spilled down her unscrubbed cheeks, but she just stood there, not even reproaching me. It was awful. Trying to fill the miserable silence, I went on: "There's a nice wool coat and several pretty dresses you can take with you for Clarice. They're very little worn, just outgrown."

At that Florence dropped onto the floor whatever she

held, and covered her face with both hands, drawing a great sob from the depths of her flesh. She wiped her eyes on her wrist, but had to turn up her apron to blow her nose. The rickrack trimming dangled from the pocket like a forlorn streamer.

She made two tries before she could get the words out, and I stood sick and embarrassed, wishing I could kick myself. "You have give me an awful lot of nice things since I come, and the work is plumb easy; but I'm *so* glad you changed your plans," she blubbered, then stopped to blow again. "Because I can't hardly stand it here no longer! It's so awful *lonesome.* I got so I juz think I *got* to go home. And find out what they're all *talkin'* about. The neighbors, and the kids, and Jim. I been worryin' myself to death how I was goin' to tell you."

She came toward me with her arms held out, but I managed to pat her shoulder and escape.

Florence sang the whole week. And during that time she never rinsed a dish nor mopped the floor, which grew so sticky around the stove your soles snapped audibly when you walked there.

Boat morning dawned dreary, with rain falling in sheets, but Florence would not wait indoors for Hazel Johnson to phone us when the boat was leaving Temperance Creek. Instead she took Clarice to the landing where they sat until they must have been soaked. Then the boat flashed down, Florence hustled Clarice on, and they were gone from our lonesomeness forever.

While I debated what now to do for help, a visitor rode in. She was Julia Reid, from the divide. Once she had stayed with our children when Len and I had to hurry out on a legal matter, and we knew what she was like.

"Mrs. Reid," my husband said without much preface,

"would you consider coming to help my wife during lambing and shearing?"

"Why, I don't know—" Mrs. Reid began in her soft voice.

"And come about the middle of February, a month before lambing begins," Len said firmly, closing the contract.

"Well now, maybe I could," Mrs. Reid said tranquilly.

Julia Reid was a widow, strong, impressively tall, and good looking. She rode well and horses liked her. She liked them too, and she liked filling hungry men with good food. Her two grown sons were still at home, and one or the other of them would also be glad to help us with our spring work.

There was another interesting thing about the Reids: though they lived on their divide ranch, they also owned Kirby Bar, the deeded land that adjoined our range on the lower or northern side. The Kirby place included plowland that might be made very productive if an irrigation dam was put in the narrow gorge from which Kirby Creek flowed. There was also a rusty orchard, a boulder-strewn pasture, and beside the creek a neglected old house.

I was very much aware of Kirby's charms, if not quite certain about its economic possibilities. The rough contour of the land on both sides of the creek made unexpected coves and rocky knolls that did not bare everything to the eye as at Kirkwood. The river inscribed a deep outward arc here, with powerful rapids at the farthest point.

On the Oregon side, across from this point, cliffs rose in thin shelves, scarcely leaving room for the trail, and since one could see but little of the gorge either north or south because of the great curve, a sense of loneliness seemed to haunt the bar. If you wanted to commit a crime,

Kirby with its secluded coves and draws would seem to be a first-rate place to select.

The Reids no longer farmed the land, and we had begun to cast thoughtful eyes on it. Its range might carry two hundred ewes, and the fields had at one time produced crops. Sometimes members of the Reid family stayed over night in the house, but their home was definitely on the divide.

Until Mrs. Reid could come, I knew I would have to get along as best I could, for to leave the ranch indefinitely with no woman in the house was unthinkable. Where only men prevail, supplies and equipment disappear, fences go, windows are broken. Ruin overtakes garden and orchard. Men who never have desserts and who never have clean clothes handed to them come to look, act, and smell a little peculiar. Women are a luxury; yet when they leave, so do profits.

It was deceptively warm, that November evening. Supper was over and the day's cares all but folded away. By the table in the best light Len read his *Pacific Wool Grower* and Bob perused old copies of *Life* and the *National Geographic,* which never palled on our bachelor help. The two boys were carrying in armloads of limbwood, which tended to escape from their hold and roll. Patsy and I had cleared the supper dishes, and with my blue platter filled with scraps I went out to feed the dogs. We now had Laddie, a tawny young shepherd, so gentle and forbearing that visiting dogs sometimes imposed on him. In the velvety dark he and Bell pretended to quarrel over their food. I turned back, enjoying the mild dusk, carrying the platter in my hand, not hurrying.

Starting down the two steps to the concrete runway, I

was blinded by the light streaming from the alcove windows and stepped on something that rolled, perhaps a piece of stovewood. If I hadn't been carrying the blue platter, I might have saved myself.

Len heard the muffled sound, and when only silence followed, he put down his paper and came out. I lay where I had fallen because I could not yet move. He gathered me up and carried me in to the padded chest.

"Patsy," he said quietly, "wet a towel with cold water and bring it here. Mother's hurt."

The boys came wide-eyed, and Bob stood up uncertainly, leaving his magazines. I could see and hear everything, but I could not speak because my head hurt so terribly. I turned over on my face and motioned to have the towel put on my neck. Len examined me with gentle hands.

"I can't find any blood, or anything wrong," he said in agitation.

For an hour I lay still, while the children stayed close and spoke in low tones. Len never left me, though there was little he could do to help. I was then put to bed, and at length I slept. In the morning I was able to dress, and with everyone lending a hand, breakfast was presently on the table.

I got through that day, and the following day was better. Nevertheless, a single spot that burned like a hot dime was developing low at the back of my head. And if I let myself become agitated the dime got hotter.

From this time on, by lying down for half an hour every afternoon I could finish the day. I could also keep school and get the house work done in a slovenly fashion. Once in a discouraged moment I thought that Something was punishing me for failing with Florence.

The children were endlessly thoughtful and good, looking mournful and disappointed only when I said I couldn't bat flies or chase grounders any more. Every night when I sank into bed, I longed for the day in February when Julia Reid would ride to my door.

For Christmas this year, I made monogrammed handkerchiefs for each of the men, choosing to do this because it was relaxing to sit and sew by hand. Patsy made chair-backs for her grandmothers. Joe was using his new Venus color pencils to draw pictures for calendars. He practiced patiently, and the scraps of paper I put into the waste-basket were covered with anatomical sections of deer and horses, hawks' wings and heads, and eagle talons fiercely curved.

The children's Christmas present for their father was an extension mirror which was to be screwed to the wall over the washbasin. When it arrived and they discovered the side that enlarged monstrously, they smirked in it at every opportunity for days. It was going to make Dad speechless with satisfaction.

Because of my languor, Christmas was a degree wistful, and Len stayed home all day, sending Dell to the camps. It was good that we had been forehanded about the Christmas shopping, for the river now began to run ice and the boat stopped. Through Christmas week I held school, but each day was harder than the one before, and by New Year's Eve, I knew I was getting to the end of my strength.

As I stood drooping, Len came and put his arms around me. "You are going out," he said. "Wouldn't you like to go to your mother's, and have a visit with her while you're getting a thorough physical check-up? It will be as easy as this: on Monday morning I'll take you across the divide. At two in the afternoon the bus goes through Lucile, and gets into Lewiston about six. You'll have supper there and then leave on the night pullman. You'll be at your mother's by breakfast time!"

A chill hand closed slowly over my heart. As long as Len thought I was just uncomfortable but would soon be all right, I could endure almost anything. But now it was clear that he thought something was very wrong.

I tried to speak casually. "You could stay here, at the house, until I get back?"

"Yes, but I won't try to teach the kids!"

"What if—what if I had to stay awhile—quite a little while?"

"Time enough to worry about that. The thing to do is make up your mind you're going, and *go*."

Len holds to the consoling belief that if you hurt but can reach the right doctor, he can give you the right pill, and you'll be okay. See the doctor, get the pill, quit feeling second-rate. It is beautifully simple.

New Years was no holiday inside the house and outside it was dolorous, for an icy wind funneled through the gorge and a gray blanket of cloud covered the canyon from rim to rim. We did a big emergency washing, and Patsy and her father hung the stiffening clothes on the line. I made bread enough to last a week if biscuits or pancakes were eaten for breakfast.

Then late in the afternoon I laid out my things to pack. The boys asked exactly when would I leave and where would I go; but Patsy said nothing. All the time that I packed she stood close, handing me this and that.

"Will the boys and I be alone with Bob tomorrow?" she asked as I closed the bag.

"Yes, you will. Dad will make it back tomorrow night if he possibly can. But if the snow is deep on top, he may be away until Tuesday some time—he'd stay with Dick

Carter. You must do things the way you think *I* would, and keep the boys cheered up. It'll be fun not having school!"

I could not meet her eyes. She longed to know exactly when I could return, so that tomorrow she could begin checking off the days; but I could not give her an honest answer. Suddenly she turned and ran downstairs. A colloquy went on below; then a door slammed.

Len came up to the bedroom. He took my hands and pressed me down on the bed, then sat beside me.

"Rest a minute. Would you think—would it be possible—couldn't you take the children with you? I'd forgot that Dell wants to go out right away—he's been planning it. I'll have to tend camp next week— Bob can't do it, you know. Any high trail makes him dizzy. What do you think about it?"

Before I spoke, I thought of a good many things. Len waited, not hurrying me. The answer would be the same anyhow.

"I guess I'd better not go."

"You've *got* to go."

"I just haven't the strength to get the kids ready—not by tomorrow morning."

"Oh, they can pack their own things!" Len cried joyfully. "And I'll get supper! But you'd better go tell Patsy yourself. Just now she went out in the cold looking absolutely sick."

I found my daughter crouched against the house, out of the wind and out of sight, her jacket pulled across her breast and her eyes carefully blank.

"Patsy, come in and help me! We're going to get you children's things ready too. You're going with me!"

"Mother! Not all of us!"

"Yes, all of you. Dad will take us across the top in the morning. He'll have Bob go out right away and bring in more horses."

"Mother," my good child asked tremulously, "can we afford it?"

"Goodness yes!" I cried heartily. I took her little hand and we started in, wrenching a few frozen pieces from the clothesline as we went.

At seven it was still cold and solitary along the creek, but we were warmly dressed, with the authority of wool and leather—heavy coats and caps, lined mittens, boots with wool socks. We rode silently, scrubbing against the brittle sumac and ducking the leafless alder branches that overhung the trail. As the light increased, so did the cold. There was no wind here, but the breath of winter seemed to brush like a hand against our faces. The crunch of hooves and the creaking of gear were the only sounds. Even the creek under its lacy ice shawl was a mere tinkle. Steam rose from the horses and hung in the still air, but in their plushy winter coats our mounts seemed indifferent to the cold.

The children and I had never ridden out in winter time; they felt subdued and I a little uneasy. Len in his wool helmet and turned-up collar jogged ahead, hunched in the saddle for warmth, and the children kept their horses in close rank behind the packmule.

In Sumac Gulch where we left Kirkwood Creek and the real climb began, it was growing lighter. Thin wreaths of snow clung to the frigid norths, and when we looked back we could see across the heads of the lower ranges the indelible cold blue of the Oregon rims. Presently along the topmost of these peaks a cold glitter ran, as the first shafts of day struck fire. The river had been lost from sight, and the great wintry sweep filled me with melancholy. There were just too many stark, unpeopled ridges, too many icy gorges between them, too much impersonal waste. I wished I were warm and busy at Kirkwood, but with no hot dime at the back of my head.

The snow was deepening in the trail, but we paused often to rest the horses. Overhead the sky was changing from gray to pale blue, not reflecting any warmth at all.

At Dick Carter's we stopped. Dick bounced out of his two-roomed cabin followed by Nellie, his little shepherd, who was carrying his gloves. It was too cold to sit long on our horses, talking, and there wasn't time to go inside.

Twice Len bade us all get down and walk to take the cold and stiffness out of our legs. By eleven o'clock we had crossed and put behind us the thinly timbered summit and now we were filing down through the snowy comb that overhung the eastern rim. On the Salmon River side of the divide it was warmer, and by noon we were riding into Slim Johnson's snug ranchyard on lower Cow Creek. Len had phoned them the night before and they were expecting us, with a hot lunch ready.

When we had eaten, Slim ran his pickup out of the shed, and the children and I got in the cab while he and Len transferred our baggage. Len came to tell me goodbye.

He said quietly: "I know everything's going to be all right. Just get fixed up and hurry back. Call me if you need me. Or—or just call me anyway!"

As we started down the road I saw him wheel his string of horses into motion, headed for the lonely divide and even lonelier Kirkwood.

Through a bright, heatless afternoon sun the bus pulled up the frosted terraces of Whitebird Hill. By this time I was dizzy and half sick, but it was not because we were swinging above the depths of Whitebird Creek. The law of averages, which my husband supported stoutly, would protect the bus on this unrailed hill. That is, the bus *could* go off, but the chances were very great that it would not, and this I should remember.

By the time we reached Lewiston the first stars had come out above the twinkling city, and I wondered if I could go any further. But a hot supper there, with many cups of coffee, saved my soul.

The doctor said carefully: "You say that neither your eyes nor your ears bled? My guess is that you have suffered a slight intercranial hemorrhage. If this happened about six weeks ago, the effects should wear off in another four or five months. I see no point in undertaking X-ray work now, but you should stay here for observation—there may be other injury."

He wrote prescriptions and then asked questions about Hell's Canyon, after which we said goodbye and I went to a beauty parlor for a permanent to raise my spirits.

I realized that some morning I must get up with a decision made, either to go back to the ranch or get Len to send the children's school things while I hunted for an apartment. I would have to decide this myself, without help from anybody. My only satisfaction would be that I had achieved this much maturity, that I had decided something far-reaching by myself. Achieving any degree of maturity is a lonely business; there's nothing gay about it.

During those days my mother appeared to enjoy her grandchildren tremendously. They followed her about, asked her countless questions, took her walking, and played her radio whenever she did not object. They were taken by the neighborhood children to visit school, and came home with mixed and excited reactions.

My medicine seemed to be efficacious; I rested; I felt a thousand percent better. But my heart was certainly not in this neat, tight little town on a busybody highway and a transcontinental railroad.

One rain-lashed evening two weeks after we arrived, Whitebird called me. The connection was weak and confused, but I was sure it meant Len. In imagination I saw the thin wires that swayed between rock-jacked telephone poles in the howling Snake gorge, while an anxious voice at the other end strove to pierce the alternate roaring and total deafness of the belled box.

I heard words, strained and ghostly: "Hello, dear."

That was all; the roaring triumphed. After an interval, Mrs. Hardin, the Whitebird operator, came on.

"I'll have to repeat for you, Mrs. Jordan," she said in her gentle drawl. "Len says 'How are you?' and the storms are increasing and the trail across the summit will close soon. The boat won't be running for quite a while, he says. So he says if you leave your mother's tomorrow night on the train, he'll phone Slim Johnson to meet your bus in Lucile the next evening."

It was a long installment, but Mrs. Hardin was an apt relayer. She waited now for my reply.

I had not expected a call; I was not ready. But I must come to a decision right now, even if it affected the rest of my life and my family's. I must have sighed, for my mother glanced up from her book by the lamp. Her look was not peremptory; she would not tell me what to do.

"Mrs. Hardin," I said, "tell him we'll be there."

Silence again.

It was a longer interval this time, but Mrs. Hardin spoke with the same correct blend of official remoteness and neighborly warmth:

"Len says to tell you he's glad that you're all right and that you're coming home, because it is mighty lonesome; and he hopes you will have an easy trip; and to stay at Johnsons' until he gets there. And he says he will bring extra coats and not to worry about crossing the top. And he says he's glad you are fine, but don't come unless the doctor says you should—and that's right, Mrs. Jordan. Don't come till you're well. And how is your mother and the children, and give your mother his love."

I replied: "Tell him we are all pretty well. No, say we are all *very* well." There was no use worrying Len with measured statements.

"You are all *very* well," Mrs. Hardin murmured before she cut me off.

And now she used her farewell voice: "Len says goodbye and God bless you."

"Tell him goodbye," I said.

Our traveling connections worked out well, and when the bus stopped at tiny, snowbound Lucile, there stood Slim in front of the store, waiting. In half an hour we were in the Johnsons' compact little house in the shelter of the creek, and the children were getting acquainted with the Johnsons' own little cowboy, who had been asleep when we came before. Peter was not a year old, but already he was the owner of made-to-order cowboy boots. Slim held them up proudly, thrusting his fingers into the sharp little toes.

Len had not arrived yet, and Slim had heard it was bad

on top. But after supper my husband phoned from Dick Carter's. He seemed to be saying he would be down in the morning.

The Johnsons gave us their loft rooms, which were reached by a surprising little stairway, and we slept there as warm and contented as kittens.

At ten o'clock next morning Len rode creaking into the frosty yard, pulling his saddlestring and packmule behind him. When he had warmed himself and visited with Slim and admired Peter, he said we must go.

Mary came out to show us the best way for wrapping a child to ride horseback in the cold, and loaned us wool blankets to do it with. She laid a blanket across Joe's saddle, the ends hanging down each side. Len lifted Joe into the saddle and Mary pulled the back fold up around his body and over his legs, so he could hold it firm with his knees. Then she brought the front fold back and tucked it tight the same way. The blanket would stay in place as long as Joe kept his legs firm against the horse.

With Steve and Patsy similarly rolled, and with a packet of Mary's sandwiches we were off, so bundled that the horses under us looked small and overworked. As the trail climbed, the wind rose and the wintry sun vanished. The timbered ridges on our left were becoming lost in a gray web of cloud, and over the bare-shouldered hill along which we rode, a lead ceiling dropped to rest. Snow began to flutter out of this ceiling, steadily, without effort, and by the time we reached Till Phillips' solitary cabin, just under the summit, the children and I were aching with cold.

But it would be still colder on top and Len made us dismount. Taking the blankets with us, we made our way in to Till's. He stoked his ancient heater red hot, and we stood so close to it that somebody's coat scorched and began to smell. Presently Till went into his other low little room and made coffee. We added Mary's sandwiches, and had a sociable lunch together. But through the small windows we could see the snow piling deeper; there were still miles of trail ahead.

As we rounded up through the snow comb to reach the summit, I heard the ominous whistling of the wind, and now it struck with stinging force. The snow was no longer falling, it was riding level on the wind. It drove into our eyes, under scarves and gloves, and up our coat sleeves. I could see one horse ahead and one behind, and sometimes the trunk of a tree, but the world was a gray cell that moved with us, spiked with black dots of snow. At intervals I called to the children, to know if they were keeping their legs wrapped, and their faint voices whipped back eerily. While they always said they were "just fine," I knew their toes and fingers were going numb.

Probably it was not over an hour until we were entering Dick Carter's lane, between the ranks of snow-burdened trees, but here the wind abated and the fine snow sifted straight down. A sense of unreality came with this quiet cold, as if we rode in a painted landscape where everything essential to life and consciousness had frozen. And until we came in sight of Dick's house, I could not shake off this odd feeling. In the field and near the barn there was no sign of activity; the house windows were blank. No dogs ran out, and so we rode on silently.

Dropping to the head of Sumac, we paused for the last gate, and I felt as if I were nearly home now. Inside the gulch warmer air enveloped us. Though the day was fading fast, the snow had stopped and we could make out the forbidding rims across the Snake. The children peeped out to see what tracks there were in the snow and to speculate on what creatures had passed.

At the foot of Sumac, Kirkwood Creek opened familiarly, and soon we were passing the boulder, big as a house, that had rolled from its base above Brownlee Hole a thousand years ago. We rode so close the jingle of bridle chains echoed from the rock. Lonely Carter Mansion showed up suddenly, then was gone. We rounded the last bend in the trail, and could see the light in our own window.

Though I could have got off my horse alone, Len lifted me down in his arms. "You're home," he said. "Everything's all right again."

In the spring we initiated a project on the creek just opposite the house; and the following fall we finished another above the tin gate, close to the mule-skeleton site. Sometimes our labors to perfect our holdings and force Nature to yield more of her benefits reminded me of Robinson Crusoe. In this period of national uncertainty we were never sure what experiments in control the government might undertake next. We expected to contribute hard work and all the foresight we were capable of, but beyond this we could prepare for the future with hardly more confidence than Robinson on his isle. In any backward-looking bewilderment over the slow recovery of the 1930's, this uncertainty is a key.

Choosing a spot where the creek was fifteen feet lower than the irrigation ditch which ran along the edge of the corral, Bob and Len set up a wheel and flumed down a head of water, to turn it. The wheel came from the rear axle of a Model-T Ford, running in the original bearings, and it connected with a generator which charged a row of storage batteries. To catch the water, large metal stock-bells

—with clappers removed—were bolted like cups to the rim of the wheel.

Electric wire from this "plant" to the house completed the work, and we would now be able to burn two more small lights and use the radio almost as much as we desired. Equally important was the fact that my washing machine could now be geared to water power, and I should be independent for ever more of the much too popular Briggs and Stratton gas engine.

The men laid a good floor and set a tent over it, with the washer and a bench for tubs at the end. Along one side Bob set up an antique heating stove with a watercoil inserted in its middle, and this connected with a fifty-gallon oil drum with a faucet. There was room on the flat top of the stove for a clothes-boiler besides.

Hired men and herders commonly did their personal laundry, sometimes awkwardly and with fantastic results; I did the washable blankets and pillowslips for all. But now I would be able to say to a man, "If you want to wash your things in the washer, let me know. You won't have to come in the house at all. I'll help you a little and we'll put it out fast."

My offer was accepted over and over—most men are *willing* to be clean. And there was another advantage: I knew something about an employee's personal worries after spending a half hour with him in the mellowing presence of steam and melted home-made soap.

THE DROP-BAND BEGAN TO MOVE TO HIGHER GRASS, and Mrs. Reid went along as Mrs. Reynolds had done, producing similar marvels of cookery under trying conditions as she went.

At Little Bar she was ready and smiling when the first shearers arrived, but only the next day her son Fred rode down from the divide to bring her crushing news. Their house had burned, and the personal possessions of years were gone. In our critical moment Mrs. Reid did not forsake us, but she came to Kirkwood, when shearing was over, in a silence and depression quite alien to her. The only thing we could offer was the indefinite use of our big square tent, and a supply of the small things without which housekeeping cannot begin anew.

This ill luck probably decided Mrs. Reid to sell us Kirby Bar. The papers were presently completed, and Kirby was ours. In the fall we would begin using it and its range.

That summer in Grangeville we stayed in an apartment and had access to a public library and also to the books and friendship of Inez Shaffer, whose husband was a druggist. Mrs. Shaffer not only loaned me *The Flowering of New England,* but also *The Nutmeg Tree.* And she was the sort of person to whom you could turn in many an odd difficulty, whether it involved pills or people.

On a September morning before we were to start back to the ranch, our landlady knocked excitedly. "I just heard it on the radio," Mrs. Scales cried. "The Germans are dropping bombs on Warsaw! It's going to start a war, they say!"

A war, we said to each other. A war in Europe! How could a war be starting anywhere without our knowing about it? We saw we must wake up and learn what was going on beneath the surface in the world beyond our national borders.

The day we were leaving for home I stopped at the office of the Grangeville *Free Press* to subscribe to the paper. It would sometimes be weeks reaching us, I knew, but in a canyon a fact keeps its color and shape a long time—its staleness or freshness is no great matter.

In his boxy little office we were greeted by Mr. Olmsted, the editor, a short man with a belligerent manner. He began filling out my subscription card, then paused.

"Why don't you send us the correspondence from that hole in the ground where you live? In return I'll mail you the paper free and supply you with stationery and postage."

"Not much happens," I said. "There'd be weeks when you'd get nothing at all."

"We don't get stuff from everybody every week. Couldn't print it if we did!" Mr. Olmsted still pretended ferocity.

"Perhaps my daughter could gather the news," I said uncertainly.

"Your daughter? How old's she?"

"Twelve."

"Twelve! Well, dammit, she can read and write can't she?"

"Yes. And I suppose writing news might be a good exercise in English."

"English! You talk as if there were schools on the river! I know better! By the way, do you realize there's a law about denying children education? Not but what anybody can teach himself, if he's a mind to."

I explained about our use of the Calvert system, and when subsequently Patsy's first batch of news was printed, Mr. Olmsted introduced it with a fullsome paragraph about our kitchen school, under a twenty-four point head.

On our way across the divide we were lucky enough to meet Mrs. Reid, and asked her if she had decided to rebuild her house. She said No, the boys had plans of their own. So we inquired if she would consider coming to Kirkwood to spend the winter, and she said she would, though it might be several weeks before she was free. She appeared pleased by the arrangement, and so were we.

With dependable help I saw I could move school to the living room, and instead of struggling to get dinner on promptly at noon, I should be able to walk downstairs when lessons were over and find everything on the table. The doctor's cautious prediction of last January had been partly realized, but the hot dime still burned at times, as a warning that Nature still regarded me as mortgaged property. Mrs. Reid's presence would mean a very different outlook for me.

On the kitchen wall I mounted a *National Geographic* map of Europe, and each day we followed the war moves as the radio newscast brought them in. It was not long before we knew more about the war than did our visitors from outside, they who read it still damp from the presses.

As soon as Mr. Russell learned we were home to stay, he hurried up from his little kingdom, which he now called "Russell Bar." He came to eat, to boast of his canning, to drop in a fresh supply of his prickly, personal innuendoes, and to tell us the latest chapter of a tale that might be called "The Gold Mine in Fourth of July Canyon." He could hardly wait to get to that story, and began it as we ate.

First he refreshed the children and me on certain facts he had related when we first knew him, about a vein of pure gold lying in a canyon known as "Fourth of July." However, there were at least four canyons so designated in the Idaho-Montana mining region, he asserted, and there was some doubt as to which was the right one.

Some years ago a certain man, not further identified, had come upon the fabulous vein of gold while fleeing from a forest fire. He was struggling down a wild and precipitous gully, crouching close to its shallow creek, even plunging into the water when the flames and smoke grew intolerable. Suddenly, there it was, a deposit of pure gold in a crevice by the water! He could see it plainly and though he dared not stay, he strove to fix the scene in his mind. When he returned months later, everything was changed and he could not find the incredible vein.

The timber was burned from the surrounding ridges; falling trees might have dammed the creek and covered the ledge. Anyhow, the heart-sick man finally abandoned his search, but before leaving he made a map of the location and was determined to return as many times as was necessary until he succeeded.

He confided the story and the map to a barber living in Michigan; the barber confided the story to Mr. Russell.

And Mr. Russell had come west partly on account of the story. During the intervening years, the first man and the barber had both died, but one of the barber's relatives knew the tale and hoped to find the map.

However, Mr. Russell believed he had sufficient data to locate the ledge himself provided he could visit all the Fourth of July canyons and eliminate the ones that did not fit the picture.

While we were out, he had at last made an exploratory trip in this connection, going with a friend who had a car.

"Did you find the ledge?" we demanded in chorus.

"No," Mr. Russell admitted, toying with his pie, "we didn't have quite time enough. We'll have to go back when we can. One more trip and I'll probably make the big strike! Golly, I may turn out to be a millionaire!"

"Where did your trip take you?" I asked.

"Well—north!" Mr. Russell was being very sly. "We'd have stayed until we found it, probably, but our grub ran out and Huffman's time was growing short. But my sakes, it was exciting!"

Gold or not, the trip had evidently done our friend much good. Considering that he had once stayed in the canyon two years without being out of it, his summer had indeed been a stirring one. I was so captivated by his enthusiasm that it was several months before it occurred to me to suspect that the mysterious ledge, the man fleeing from the fire, the barber and the map were all one grand fairytale.

During his call Mr. Russell came down to earth sufficiently to examine our wall map, but we did not discuss world events at any length. Mr. Russell was always receiving weird data about celebrated people and their motives, eccentric items no one else had yet heard. And if my views on the matter did not coincide with his more authoritative ones, or with the *presumable* views of his hero, Dr. Townsend of the Townsend Plan, a good deal of spluttering ensued. Such exchanges always ended, however, with Mr. Russell's implication that though I was in the wrong I probably meant well. So today we soon left the larger world for canyon news and gossip, a field in which our visitor's knowledge was both rich and uncanny.

"Patsy, do you want to take me to the head of Cow Creek?" Len asked his daughter at breakfast. "I want to leave this morning. You'll ride Bessie. Coming back you'll have to lead Eagle and a mule. See if Mother can spare you."

Patsy had never been tried alone on the trail with horses. She looked at me breathless.

I tried to make my nod a bright one.

She wore a small black sombrero over her yellow bob, with a wool jacket, a blue T-shirt, and new denim slacks, and she sat her horse easily and neatly. Bessie stood tall, a well-meaning undistinguished mare. I watched them round the bend in the trail with a feeling that if I did not worry a little all the time Patsy was gone, I should be failing her.

On the return she would have to dismount at gates, and each time she must manage the lead rope so as not to catch her foot in it as she swung onto her horse. Suddenly I remembered a woman down the river who was accustomed to leading a packstring but who had lost her thumb one day in a loop of rope when a packhorse sawed back.

Noon came; afternoon came and finally passed. As dusk closed in, I admitted that I felt uneasy. I reminded myself that Len never expected anything of the rest of us that we could not encompass. He took no chances himself and allowed no one else to do so.

It was only a little later that Patsy rode in. She took care of her three horses and came to the house, her manner both calm and electric. She had done it!

Babe had been running free on the range all summer, for her stiffening knees were making her nearly impossible as a mount. Whenever she was assigned to me, I walked half of the time, for the thought of her poor knees was as hard to endure as her jolting gait on a down slope. A government stallion had been running on the same range as Babe, and when I saw how well she looked the first time she drifted down to the ranch that fall, I felt a great elation. A few days later I asked Len what he thought about Babe.

He smiled. "You're seeing what you want to see. Babe's just full of good bunchgrass. She's gone barren too long."

I did not give up, and I managed to see the mare often, for she began to graze along the creek where the men were building the new dam, just below the Carter field. This dam was a part of Len's plan to try shed lambing on a small scale here. A supply of running water would be necessary in the shed, and in the outside enclosures too. The shed would be a simple framework covered with removable canvas, the floor space cut into small pens with a central alley.

While they had the time, Len and Bob cleared the whole meadow, so that it could be used for other stock when the sheep moved higher. Our cow, the same Brownie that rode up on the boat that first spring, longed for shade and grass during the arid weeks of July and August; and here, if the pasture was kept green, she could find both.

The shed was completed rapidly, Bob doing much of the work. The little parks were fenced; the main ditch was made ready. The ewes, when they saw all this, would doubtless approve. Still in a constructive mood, the men also cleared and fenced the rocky bar lying between our upper field and the river. Waste irrigation water from the field could be diverted over this area and keep its sparse grass growing. The canyon yielded with so little grace to being tidied up that any gains along this line seemed to constitute a victory.

That winter was as easy and as happy as any we had ever experienced. With Mrs. Reid's tranquil aid in the kitchen I could give school all the time it needed. We kept house better, read more, looked ahead with greater hope. Christmas was unusually cheerful, for Mrs. Reid's two sons came to dinner, Dell was in, Mr. Russell did not fail us, and Bob had postponed his layoff. For me that Christmas there was an extravagant surprise under the Christmas tree, a new portable typewriter, a gift from my husband.

January came in mild, and Dell went outside for his layoff. Dell came home sick—sick and weary of towns, hotels and the war talk. The cobwebby bunkhouse probably seemed a haven.

I brought quinine and the fever thermometer.

"You're to go to bed, and you don't need much to eat," I asserted.

"Okay," he said meekly, swallowing the fat quinine capsules. However, by the next day he thought he had been humored long enough, and came to the house at meal time. He could not eat, though, and his temperature stayed up. For another day he sat in hunched silence. Then I remembered the merits of flaxseed and lemon tea, and made up a pitcherful. Dell drank it like an obedient child, with the willing assistance of the children. Whereupon, he improved rapidly and was soon back with his packstring.

Then on a spring morning sorrowful with squalls of rain, and wreaths of fog caught on the canyon pinnacles, we suddenly had visitors. It was Fred Reid and the Reids' neighbor on the divide, Jim Davis. Jim desired to buy the Reids' home ranch, and the rest of us moved out of the kitchen so the two men and Mrs. Reid could talk business unhindered. When they had agreed, they called Len down to write them a contract.

Len produced his law book—in the canyon you may have to be your own lawyer as well as your doctor and barber—and dictated an agreement which the new typewriter turned out in impressive triplicate. A pen was brought, signatures were affixed, and the sale was complete.

I looked at Mrs. Reid to see if she were feeling depressed over selling the last of her property, especially on a sodden day like this. But she seemed mildly excited about what this would mean to her future, and what she would do with the money. When I asked her if she had any definite plans along this line, she said smiling that she would like to have an apartment house in town.

As spring advanced I had become more certain about Babe, and Len finally conceded that she was probably with foal. She was more beautiful than ever, but her disposition suffered, and I suppose she wondered why on earth she longed so to kick and bite other horses.

"Don't get your hopes up. She may not make it," Len warned me.

"Don't tell the children that," I begged. They were more excited over Babe's prospects than if she had been a member of the family.

In school Joe had reached the momentous three-day English paper, and the choice of a subject was again before us. We had been reading the story of Chief Joseph the Younger, who led the Nez Perces in the war of 1877, the last Indian war in Idaho history, and Joe chose this to write about.

No schoolboy hears the Joseph story without a tightening heart, for Joseph executed a military movement so skillful it is still studied. He led the Nez Perces on a fourteen-hundred-mile retreat from the Salmon River to the Canadian border in Montana, living as best they could in hostile territory, carrying their wounded and all the people of the tribe, from the very young to the very old, and fighting a running battle the while with United States regular troops. The flight lasted six months. It began in the hot Salmon Canyon; it ended in November snow in the mountains.

Joe illustrated his paper with a map of Joseph's route, and with sketches of wigwams and weapons. His labors brought him what Pat's had brought her, praise and a gold star from faraway Baltimore, and from his father a silver dollar.

"Come quick, Mother! Babe's in the pasture on the bar. She's kind of crying and she can't get up." It was Patsy calling me, and we had just had breakfast. Only Bob was at the ranch with us, so I dropped everything and ran with the children to the new pasture. "She's dying," I thought as I ran.

"There's nothing we can do," I explained when I saw her, "but Joe can find Bob and ask him to come as soon as he can. We must stay away. If she sees or hears people around it will make her very nervous."

At recess the children ran down fearfully. Babe still lay on the ground, still thrashing about. Bob said to the children, "I'll stay around. You go back now."

They reported the situation to me.

"Bob didn't seem worried?" I asked.

"Oh no," they said. "He just grinned."

At noon when they went down they did not stay long, but came tearing back in ecstasy. Babe's colt had come . . it was lying beside her . . it had a cute little brown head with a black nose and a stubby black mane and tail. It had the most beautiful big eyes!

I dropped everything and hurried back with them, for I could not stay away either. I found Babe looking hardly at all wearied, but very jumpy and indignant if anyone came within twenty feet of her.

"We could bring her something to eat," Patsy proposed.

"She's doing okay," Bob said, grinning.

"What are we going to name him?" Joe asked.

I made my answer with care, to get it on the record. "Babe is mine, so her colt is mine too. I'll give up my half of Bessie's colt to Patsy, but this one is mine and I'll name him myself. His name is Mercury."

Mercury! Remembering their much-conned mythology, and the wing-footed messenger about whom test questions were likely to center, the children's eyes crinkled. They said it was a nice name. But I had doubts as to how it would be received by our men. Their rule was that no animal's name should have more than two syllables—the better to call it—and one syllable was preferable. "Mercury" would soon turn into "Merc," if the name stuck at all.

By the day's end the colt was standing firmly on his four stilt legs, as bonny a sight as Babe herself. When he sought to nurse, Babe jerked around and squealed at him. But he caught hold and pushed rudely into her flank. She cried, but he did not give up until he had what he wanted.

By the next day she seemed to know that he belonged to her in some special way, and that he fully intended to be fed. Before long she was as proud of him as we were, and very jealous too. Only one big moment remained—when Dad would be told the wonderful news!

The children were all growing dependable about horses, and I was not surprised one morning when Len phoned from Lucile that he would like Joe to meet him at Dick Carter's with two horses, leaving Kirkwood around one o'clock.

Joe did his own saddling up, with Bob to okay the cinches, and stopped to tell me goodbye. He was not yet ten, our darkest, quietest child, one who seemed to get most of his rights without insisting on them. And as he mounted Buck, a good-natured new five-year-old, I noted that his face was losing its curves, changing to a long oval, and the bones of his body were going to be long rather than big.

As the horses disappeared around the bend I decided that if all went well Joe would be back with his father by seven or eight o'clock.

At eight the phone rang. It was Joe and he said he was at Dick's and had had no trouble. "But Dad hasn't come, Mother. I think I'd better start home," he finished anxiously.

"No, Joe. You must stay at Dick's until Dad comes."

"Maybe he isn't coming tonight. Then I'll have to go to bed—"

Ah, that was it. He would have to go to bed with Dick. He would rather ride home alone through the dark than sleep with someone not belonging to our family.

I was firm. "Dad will expect you to be there, whether he comes tonight or in the morning. Have you eaten supper yet?"

"Dick said we'd better wait a while longer."

At noon the next day Len and Joe rode in, Joe eager to tell me exactly how Dick fried his breakfast potatoes. You must have lots of grease in a big skillet, and it must be very hot. You must turn the potatoes in a solid sheet and only once; you must never, never stir them.

When we were alone Len said, "I was so tired and blue when I got to Dick's last night! They were just sitting down to supper, and it was so good to see Joe there, getting along well with Dick, that I felt better right away. Dick wants him to come up and spend a few days the first time he can."

As spring advanced, all schedules tightened. Using the lambing shed made our losses lighter, but Len studied ways to improve on the experiment another year. Mrs. Reid left to follow the dropband, but my crowd did not entirely fall away, and sometimes Patsy had to put aside her own school work to aid Steve. And once in a while school took the count altogether.

One Saturday morning Ed rushed in desperately, looking for Len, who was gone. He said excitedly, "I've got a bad toothache, and I've had it for three days and nights! I'm going to go out on this boat and have a dentist pull it," he finished.

"Ed," I said, "you mean you'll walk off and *leave* your sheep?"

"Not me," Ed said. "I'm not that kind of a sheepherder. I mean *somebody's* got to *take* my sheep."

I called Bob in. The sheep were only an hour away, and it was not a full band. Bob stared thoughtfully at the floor, then said, "I guess I can take 'em!"

I well knew he abhorred trails, and his stomach barely tolerated woman-cooking. What would his own cooking in camp do to him! Nevertheless he was offering to meet the emergency. He and Ed were starting off together when blessed relief came. Len rode in accompanied by an extra man. Now Ed could catch the boat as it went down.

When that was settled, I returned to the scouring and cleaning that had been neglected during the lambing rush. If you scour and clean in the *presence* of your canyon cook, she will leave and never come back; you must do it when she goes to camp.

As I labored at my tasks, Patsy was calmly calling for the last-minute news at all the ranches we could reach by phone, then typing each item slowly. While Ed was eating a little snack, I stopped to write the grocery order, the drugstore order for Bob's medicine, wrapped the books for return to the state library, looked up socks in the Montgomery Ward catalogue and put them on the order blank, and started a box of canned fruit for Hazel Johnson to the boat landing. Hazel was short on apricots, I was short on plums; we were exchanging jar for jar.

The boat was coming! The wind was right and I could hear the sound of the engines beating back and forth across the gorge. The children ran down through the field to get the mail.

They brought the letters, the newspapers, the smaller packages, and dumped them on the table. The flood spread over the table, some of it cascading to the floor. A letter in an unexpected hand startled me, and I opened it first. It was from a friend I had not seen for a long time, a professor's wife in a university town.

> ". . . The week commencement is over George and I are leaving the campus for our vacation . . . We have always dreamed of visiting you in your little paradise . . . perhaps do a little writing while we are there . . . don't want you to go to any special trouble. We just want something simple. We should love to sleep under a tree . . . so much rather visit you than go to Europe, the way things are! . . ."

A picture of the Collinses asleep under a tree, with a rattlesnake studying their neatly folded garments lying across the nearest boulder, crossed my mind and I laughed aloud. It was fortunate that McGrady would not be bringing passengers or freight after commencement time.

But somebody was at the door, and I sobered fast. It was Andy Eatmon, who had trapped on our range before; and with him was a slender girl that he introduced as his wife. He carried their bags, and his wife held the leashes of two dignified hounds.

"We want to keep house at Carter Mansion," Andy explained. "Len wrote that he could use me during the spring, so if it's all right, we'll hike right up there."

It was all right in every possible way. Tall, dark-eyed, soft-spoken and conscientious, Andy seemed to have all the virtues known to man, and had apparently picked a wife made in the same manner.

During the weeks the Eatmons stayed, the bobcats in particular lived a harried life, or ceased to live at all. We were happy that Andy had a knack for getting cats, for they were an even greater menace that spring than coyotes.

Whenever Andy was at home Joe and Steve haunted the Carter place, and Patsy loved to go up for a visit with Mrs. Eatmon, who was gentle and companionable. Moreover, if I was too hard pressed, the young woman came down to lend a hand.

For bobcat bait Andy used something none of our other trappers had tried—sturgeon meat. Evidently it worked, for our first marking, at Kirby Bar came off at one hundred twenty-eight percent.

It was a day of steady rain, better for the poor lambs, not so good for markers, and long after dark the men straggled in for supper, wet and weary.

But there was some of Andy's sturgeon to eat! Sturgeon should be fried crisp in yellow cornmeal, seasoned well, and kept sizzling hot until it is served. Mr. Russell had sent me a basket of dandelion greens, and these, with hot yeast rolls and the sturgeon made the men imagine they were almost dining out.

Because of the rain the radio reception was clearer, and when the men had eaten and perked up, they could stand the newscast better. Germany had taken Denmark and occupied the southern cities of Norway. Then I reported on the Kiplinger letter of the week, which predicted that the United States would be in the war in another year. The men made much or little about this depending on their nature.

On the next Friday afternoon, a visitor unlike any we had ever entertained before rode to the ranch. It was a woman census taker. Though she had crossed the divide on a horse, Mrs. Eva Canfield could not be confused with the genus cowgirl. She was more like a fox-hunting Englishwoman adjusting herself to an unrefined landscape. She wore a woman's town hat—not a sombrero—over her blond waves; a delicate scarf, a dressy jacket; and trousers, not levis. She made herself known to us, and after a nap, for which she confessed she was ready, she changed from trousers to skirt and came to the kitchen to visit while I prepared supper. Her comments on the food, when it was served, were edifying to me, for in the canyon, it is only sheepherders that praise the food. Even a loving husband when asked, "Was the pie good?" will counter lamely: "Sure! I'd have told you if it wasn't!"

I advised Mrs. Canfield that we had already been officially enumerated by a man census taker and she could do nothing more for us; but she said quietly that she was supposed to get the families *beyond* Mr. Newman's reach. So she would like to catch the boat in the morning and go as far up the canyon as it would take her. She was the only woman enumerator in the county, and I got the impression that she hardly needed employment and might be enumerating for the pleasure of it. Or to show up any chicken-hearted male workers. I gathered she might be about seventy years old, though she appeared much younger.

Going up by boat, Mrs. Canfield tabulated the Sheep Creek and Johnson Bar inhabitants and inquired of these people about the dwellers at Granite Creek. They were now the Allen Wilsons, the Hibbses having sold out.

I was sorry to have Mrs. Canfield go back across the hill, but she nimbly mounted her horse and was off up the Kirkwood trail, not to return.

One event made shearing slightly nervewracking this time, a crashing thunder storm. Thunder in the canyon is terrifying at any time, for in its headlong drive earthward, the lightning picks the high points at the ends of ridges, and the dark gorge is alive with rolling reverberations that never come to an end. Fortunately, the storm presently passed on; and Lucky Jordan suffered very little.

After Mrs. Reid returned to the ranch her son Fred came for her, and she told me that she was leaving not only Kirkwood but the divide as well. The apartment house for which she yearned had been found in Grangeville. Julia Reid had lived in the Snake-Salmon region since her girlhood, had married here and borne her large family, yet she seemed able to sever its ties with less pain than I would probably feel on leaving; and I was a mere adventurer here.

Now there would be only a little delay until trailing time, and a bear took full advantage of this interval, perhaps seeking to restore some balance in nature that Andy Eatmon had upset in his war on bobcats. At any rate, when Len went to Kenneth Ryan's camp next time, there was little camp left, and Kenneth was getting pretty hungry.

Kenneth was a slight, reticent boy with Irish coloring and a great aptitude for attending to his own affairs. Several days before while he was out with his sheep, a bear took possession of the tent, as its tracks plainly showed. It ate up or destroyed everything it found. It evidently knew about jam, for it bit the top off a Mason jar. It put a big tooth through Kenneth's nested aluminum cups, making them rather useless, and it turned the stove upside down. It ate the bacon, poured sourdough around, and carried off the sack of flour, leaving a powdery trail.

Kenneth assumed that the beast's curiosity must be satisfied, but that it would want lamb next, so he resolved to put all his efforts into watching the sheep. He salvaged what food he could—he would stand by of course, though the camptender's visit was several days away.

But Kenneth misjudged the bear, as he found the next evening when he returned to the tent. The guest had been back; it had torn Kenneth's bed to ribbons. The only thing to be thankful for was that he himself had not been in the bed.

On the third day Kenneth was waiting with a .303 British army rifle from the bunkhouse arsenal. He had tied up his dogs while he waited, and the two-hundred-pound brown bear walked out of the timber and started for the tent with no premonitions. Kenneth pulled down on it, and when the beast was fifty yards away he fired. The bear came right on.

Kenneth kept cool and fired again, but it took a third shot to bring the bear down. The hide would have been of little value anyhow, and Kenneth was filled with relief even if his stomach was empty.

All this was nothing much to an adventurous fellow like Kenneth, but it proved my favorite pronouncement, that sheepherders, far from being "crazy," are as sharp as anybody—they don't keep on herding if they aren't. They have to be smart to be trusted with the live gold tied up in twelve to fifteen hundred sheep; and herders are faithful to the point of self-sacrifice and risk of life.

A few days after Kenneth's trouble, Dell rode into Harry Krebbs' camp to find him sitting up at night by his fire because he had no bed! Two days before conscientious Harry had decided he ought to sleep closer to the sheep. So the big, lean boy put his bedroll on his skittish mare, laying it loosely across the saddle. But the mare took fright at something and ran away, bucking off the bed. It fell over a cliff and stuck in the rocks where only a man on a rope could retrieve it. Therefore until a new bed came, Harry would sleep sitting by a fire.

And so passed the spring. It was nearly trailing time again when the mail brought an exciting proposal for Patsy and Joe. This was an invitation from their Jordan grandparents to go with them on a two weeks' trip to San Francisco to see the fair.

It was an opportunity not to be missed, no matter how difficult the arranging might be; and by the following weekend we were ready to leave. The plan was for me to go to my mother's, taking the three children. Patsy and Joe would be picked up there; Steve and I would remain until the party returned.

Our trip down the river with McGrady, who now had a bigger boat, was eventful in only a minor way. I was in the pilothouse myself when there began a regularly spaced tapping noise. It seemed to come from the engines, and though not loud it was persistent and had a metallic note. On the up trip McGrady had had engine worries his passengers did not know about, and now as the strange noise rose and fell, his wind-burnt face turned rather greenish.

In his time on the river he had had boats sink and boats burn; he had hung up on a rock one wintry night for an agonizing period of cold and darkness. But no passenger of his had ever got more than a bump on the head, and the mail had always gone through, eventually. McGrady might seem reckless, yet he always pulled out just ahead of disaster.

At this moment he looked as if this last attack on his peace of mind was too much. From his alarm I took alarm myself, but it was no time to harry a distracted man with questions, so I located my children and waited.

Then a sudden smile lighted the pilot's face. He leaned out the open window beside the wheel and addressed a woman tourist sitting below. She was resting comfortably against the metal siding, her hair flying in the warm wind and her sweater blowing back.

"Lady," McGrady said, "would you please fasten your sweater?"

"Yes," she said, "but why?"

"It's the buttons," the captain explained.

The lady acquiesced and the tapping stopped.

At five the children and I were in Lewiston, where we cashed a check with Grocer Ruth Sapp and barely caught the bus. By ten-thirty that night we were rolling into Pendleton, where we had waited for Grandpa, over seven years before, to go on with him to the ranch that we knew about only in letters. Patsy and Joe remembered the time clearly, but Steve had been only a baby and was deprived of this jolly memory.

Though they had not eaten since noon, the children waited patiently while I scouted for a hotel. We went up to our rooms, freshened our canyon look—it is an honest, naive, baked look—and before the hour was out we were sitting up to hamburgers at a counter. Kirkwood seemed as far away as another continent.

On the first day that we could shop I bought new outfits of clothing for Patsy and Joe, of the kind we assumed were correct in a great city, quite aware that if they were not entirely right the good grandparents would fill in the gaps.

Len and I were deeply grateful for this favor for the older children; and Steve, a sometimes too generous and forgiving child, was not in the least envious.

# 15

OUR SUMMER RANGE HAD BEEN CHANGED, AND WE went into this new region for our outing. We drove to the end of a Forest road that distressed me more than any I had ever been on. It looped from Selway Falls on the Selway River to the Indian Hill lookout, by way of a shelf scraped out of a mountain as bare as the side of a china cup. Len was bent strictly on the business of getting the heavily loaded car where it was going, and I did not mention feeling uneasy.

When a hairpin turn put me on the outside of the one-way road, I could look straight into the Selway Gorge, hundreds of feet below, too deep for the roar of the river to reach me. Across this gorge along a similar ridge was a similar road, except that this ridge was timbered. If something happened over there—if the engine killed and the brake did not hold, or if the rim crumbled or the steering gear failed or a tire blew out—a car would have some chance of lodging against a tree, even if it missed a few on the way down. I was glad when we left the edge of the world and branched off to the lookout.

That night we camped out, Dell coming with horses after dusk. All the next day we rode or walked, into a silent land that raised gradually toward the Bitterroots, across which Chief Joseph had led his fugitive tribe. After dark we reached Kenneth Ryan's camp.

With us on the trip was John Hess, a high-school boy who had hitch-hiked in from his home in Oregon to try our isolation. Including Dell, there were eight people to be served from Kenneth's limited dishes.

Early in the morning we were on our way again. From a rocky shelf we looked into a verdant basin with scattered patches of spruce. Out of the timber we suddenly saw twenty elk advancing majestically, unaware of human eyes. We watched until they disappeared again.

"Sometimes I've seen a hundred at once from here," Dell said, quietly.

By one o'clock in the afternoon we were fording icy Buck Lake Creek. The men unpacked the camp and built me a fire. Then everybody but me broke out his fishing gear, and within an hour I was serving mountain trout.

We stayed on this creek a week, an idyllic period even though the cooking for seven people must be done on an open fire. Every morning we fished, and when the sun was at its highest we went into the clear pools for a shivering dip.

At night giant porcupines visited us. One ate a leg from John's pants, and the leather laces from his boots, which sat only a few inches from John's sleeping face.

During all his waking hours John carried across his suntanned back a long yew-wood bow he had made; and the next night he astounded everybody by shooting a porcupine out of a tree that overhung camp. Now John had heard that an unarmed man lost in a forest could survive on porcupine flesh, assuming he could locate such a beast and knock it over with a club. To verify this truth, he asked me to boil one of the slain porky's legs.

I boiled it ten hours, after which it was still as tough as saddle-leather, and we did not seem to have proved much.

John shot game birds too, and when these were well stewed and the juice thickened, they made great eating, especially when Len baked biscuits by means of a reflector to go with the gravy.

With regret we left Buck Lake Creek, for the lambs must soon be sold, and I must talk to Mrs. Reynolds about coming in for the winter.

The wethers brought seven and a half cents, and the ewe lambs nine and a quarter cents, and Len felt he had done well enough. The chief cloud on our horizon was the likelihood of war. Many young men had enlisted; more would go. Old men, men with bad hearts or bad knees, cannot herd sheep on canyon range, and we might find ourselves herding our own sheep, Len warned.

Our lambs were at last approaching the type he desired, fast-maturing, with a wool not coarsened too much in the cross. Previously he had tried Leicester, Suffolk and Delaine bucks on our basic Rambouillet stock. This year he had tried a new buck, the Panama, which is a Lincoln-Rambouillet cross. The results looked good so far, but if this judgment proved premature, Len would try something else.

On the first of September Len took us to the top of the divide. No one had come with horses, so we left all our things with good-natured Till, and the children and I walked home. It gave me a catch in my throat to realize this might be the last time I returned to Kirkwood at summer's close. By next fall Patsy would be ready for high school, Joe for the seventh grade, Steve for the fifth, and we must make this last year really count.

Once more Patsy took up her *Free Press* correspondence, and her first news was a young reporter's dream. A rider on the trail had found a corpse floating in our Halfmoon eddy. He phoned the sheriff, who dispatched two men on horses to recover the body. They told us the victim had been stabbed, in some fracas far up the river, and had come down through Hell's Canyon.

The first night the men got only as far as our house, so they laid their burden on the hayrack for safekeeping, and spent the night with us. The dead man lay there alone in his canvas wrap as night came down, and the children went out and walked around the hayrack thoughtfully. They had never been close to a dead man before, and this man did not even have a name.

In the morning our visitors rode on. Only Bob and the children kept me company, and the rain fell mournfully. Bob developed an alarming pain in his abdomen, and I hurried to read up the symptoms of appendicitis and prepared to start phoning for help or getting horses ready.

But Bob refused to be ill and went about his chores, though he must have been miserable. Toward evening, while he was carrying a bucket of grain somewhere, he suddenly remembered a poor old ewe with a sore back, one that had been lost and left behind when the bands went out. Quickly he wedged the bucket of grain into a low tree-crotch while he went to treat the ewe.

There was twelve pounds of the grain; and a few minutes

later Brownie, our cow, passed this spot. We knew Brownie loved green apples uncontrollably, and if a bar of soap was left within reach she always ate it. Evidently grain was her third weakness.

When Bob returned a little barley scattered on the ground told him the story. By this time Brownie had lain down, sighing faintly as she prepared to swell. At bedtime her eyes had a glazed look and she breathed loudly. I went to the corral at three o'clock in the morning and found that she had not moved. Her great bulk flowed out around her, fawn colored and silky, her skin undeniably stretched. She looked as if there was twice as much of her as there should be. But she was groaning only a little.

Cows have less sense of humor than any other farm animal, yet in the light of my lantern Brownie appeared to flick her nearest ear and smile, as if implying that an occasional indiscretion was good for anybody.

The next day it rained and Bob could not work much, but like Brownie he was feeling better. Len phoned from Grangeville that it would be October before he could bring Mrs. Reynolds in to help me. Life in the canyon seemed to have stopped. Only outside was anything happening, and that was not very good. The radio reported ominous news: Japan had signed a treaty with Italy and Germany, from which the United States was expected to take warning.

I was glad to find that groundcherries, citron and cucumber pickles needed immediate attention, and I remembered the green tomato preserves that Mr. Russell was always yearning for, made with brown sugar and many lemons.

Having both the brown sugar and the lemons, I began on these preserves at once. They required several days of alternate boiling and cooling to get the desired texture.

and the finished product was so dark the children at once named it "tar." Mr. Russell came up that afternoon and I invited him to take a taste.

"And if you'd like a pint, it's yours," I added.

He took a cautious bit on the end of a teaspoon, narrowed his eyes and laughed deprecatingly.

"No, no, I wouldn't say you quite got it," he declared finally. "But if you made that jar for me, oh, I'll take it. Now Mrs. Kitchen's green tomato preserve, it was thick all right, but it was *light* colored. She just couldn't keep any of it in the house!" Mrs. Kitchen was a paragon with whom he had once boarded, and we often heard of her.

Notwithstanding, Mr. Russell came up a few days later and said, "Like I told you, your green tomato preserve isn't like Mrs. Kitchen's, but if you've got any more you can't get rid of, I'll take it off your hands."

But the children implored me not to give away any more tar—they promised to eat it all.

And now Mrs. Reynolds finally came. Bob took Eagle over for her to ride, and Buck for Len. They stopped by Dick Carter's to say Hello. Dick had heard that the Nazis were seizing control in French Guiana.

"Len," he said anxiously, "maybe you and me better enlist. Somebody's got to go stop the Nazis!" He pronounced Nazi the way Winston Churchill said it on the radio, with a flat, nasty *a* and a nauseating *z*.

"Dick's a game old rascal," Len told me. "He'd stop 'em or die trying! Have you heard about what happened to him? Well, he was at Lucile loading winter supplies on his packhorse, and a mule that was standing there kicked him just behind the ear. When somebody got to Dick, he was out cold, with a hole in his skull the exact size and depth of a mule-shoe calk. They loaded him into a car and took him to the hospital in Grangeville.

"The next morning he waked up early, and his mind was as clear as could be. He figured out where he was and got up. He found his clothes in a cupboard and got out of the hospital without anybody seeing him. On the highway he thumbed a ride, and by the time the nurses missed him he was back in Lucile, loading up his horse again. He said he couldn't gain anything by staying in the hospital, and it cost money besides. But that dent looks like it isn't going to come out."

It didn't. I saw it later in all its delightful horror.

It was a busy winter, now that Patsy must put in afternoon as well as morning hours on her lessons. In English we were dreaming through Washington Irving's *Alhambra;* in grammar it was participles and gerunds, as well as diagramming, of which I thoroughly approved. In arithmetic we did the cubic contents of cylindrical tanks, and tried to reason the evils and advantages of installment buying. In English history we read of Charles II's beheading, and in the history of architecture we were solemnly distinguishing Renaissance from Gothic.

With a little slack time in January, Len began drawing plans for the house we hoped to build when we moved to a town with a high school. We felt we must have a considerable tract to place the house on, for how, after living in a canyon, could we squeeze ourselves onto a small lot with neighbors so close they might hear us breathe? Our ideal home would have acreage close enough to town so the children could reach school without riding a bus, a view, and room enough to keep horses.

From the first days of our marriage, Len and I had dreamed of a stone house, and now discovering *Houses of Stone* by Frazier Forman Peters, we had all the encouragement we needed. We decided to settle in Grangeville, which had the most complete high school in the county, but what building stone was available there we did not know. (Eventually we hauled basalt from the Salmon River Canyon. The five-sided columns break with a gentle-rounded cleavage, and the crystalline shape makes a nice design when faced in concrete.)

That spring there were more people than usual at our table, more men coming and going, more excursionists on the river. Our hired help returning from layoffs invariably brought colds or flu with them, but it was hard to feel vexed when you saw how willingly they committed themselves to a corner of the bunkhouse and consented to be fussed over.

In the old cabin—and we did not know its age or how many times its floor had been replaced—no exhausted returnee gave a second thought to the ghost of David Kirk who had died there. Kirk, it was said, had been a rather intemperate man, and could often be found in the bunkhouse "sobering up on canned tomatoes." One wintry night having indulged a little deeper than usual, he became obsessed with the idea that something was after him, something that was "rolling up high behind him," and he went dashing barefoot up the snowy trail to escape it. He had gone a good ways before he was found half frozen and brought back; and presently pneumonia carried him off.

His funeral, with a burial service read by the ranch owner's wife, may have been the only one ever held at

Kirkwood; his marble stone on the upper side of our south field was the only one I ever saw in the canyon, though there were numerous graves.

But we had our share of misfits too. Among the fifteen at the table during lambing was a pallid young fellow about whom we had been told only that he was willing to work anywhere, but especially *in the canyon.* He took the shunned night shift and seemed anxious to do his work well, but in his limited contacts with the rest of the crew, he talked with no one, and a whisper went around that he had recently completed a prison term.

Since he was in the bunkhouse by day, when all the other men were gone, and only women and children around, he was on my mind a good deal. Something about his sickly coloring suggested to my evil mind that his wrong-doing might be of a social nature, an idea as persistent as it was unjustified by evidence.

At five each afternoon he came to the house for his supper and to pick up his midnight lunch, but he remained wholly silent, as if by preference. After that I saw no more of him until he came for his belated breakfast. I felt I must keep alert, and see that at all times he was treated exactly like everyone else.

But now the other men who slept in the bunkhouse began to miss small things they had left in their duffelbags, and one night somebody turned out the pale young fellow's possessions and found all the missing articles, as well as such pathetic things as worn ranch towels and pillowslips.

Someone confronted him with this evidence, and he came in and demanded his check. He hurried off across the hill with a bitter expression, and I could not bear to think about him afterward. It was clear that canyons do not cure everything.

Patsy was fourteen, and no longer a little girl. She had ceased to be Patsy and was now Pat. We adapted ourselves to this change as fast as we could, and had accepted it in time to have the right name tooled into the cantle of the saddle that Ray Holes of Grangeville was making for her. The saddle was our way of recognizing that she had finished grade school.

It arrived by boat, and Pat's eyes were starry when it was placed on Bessie, who boasted Arabian blood, but probably did not realize how she was being honored. Pat would have preferred to try the saddle on Lad, Bessie's rascal of a colt. He was regarded as Pat's property, and she had been on his back; but he was in need of thorough breaking by an expert. The saddle had that pungent tan-bark smell and golden satin feel that drives hired men and eighth-grade girls crazy, and everybody went out to caress it.

Gone that morning was Lark Alkire, a strong, compact fellow in his fifties, good natured but not fanciful; he had returned again this spring to help through lambing. He came not altogether for the wages, but partly because he liked the canyon and sheep.

Len had directed him to round up some stray ewes and lambs and get them to what was left of the drop-band, miles away in the forks of Steep Creek, where Dell was in charge. Meanwhile Len and Ed Fick were marking Ed's band at Big Bar.

Three days after Lark was due in Steep Creek, Dell became anxious and dispatched a boy to Big Bar to find out why Lark had not come.

Along the route that Lark would presumably follow there was a small supply camp. So Len took Ed and Kate and set out immediately for it. On the way they saw the stray lambs, and with misgivings they pushed on to the camp, which was not much farther.

In the tent they found Lark lying on his back in a pitiable state of neglect and nerves. He was weak and in pain, but he could talk. He said that three days before while trying to get his sheephook on a wiry lamb, he had twisted his back and fallen to the ground paralyzed. He had managed to drag himself to the camp, but it had taken hours. And in the tent there was nothing but some rice and a can of water.

Though it cost agony to move, he had managed to cook some rice, using up all the wood within reach. From then on he had lain and waited. There was no way to signal for help; no one had passed near.

Something must be done at once, and there was little to work with. Lark was too heavy for two men to carry any distance, and he could not ride a horse. Though the river was only three *miles* away, it was thirty-five hundred *vertical* feet down. Fortunately the *Florence,* McGrady's new big boat, was due tomorrow—that much was good.

They would have to use a travois or "squaw buggy," Len decided. It was lucky they had Kate, for she was probably the only mule or horse on the outfit that would pull a travois.

Len and Ed cut two poles and lashed blankets between them to form a litter. At one end they secured the poles to either side of Kate's packsaddle; the opposite ends would drag on the ground. Because of the angle of the hill, however, Lark would have to *face* Kate, and brace himself with his feet, just as much as he could, against her rump.

From the tent he watched the men do a trial run, Ed acting as the paralyzed victim, and by the time everything was ready, poor Lark was finding it almost funny. The travois appeared tenable, but Kate would have to be headed straight down the hill, and there would be none of the "traverse" that skiers can employ.

Big Lark was hoisted on, and the journey began. After enduring days of pain, hunger and moments of panic, Lark was not critical of the form of rescue. It took three hours of bumping and stalling, with rests for Lark and rests for Kate, but with cigarettes to smoke and relief in sight, Lark had recovered a good deal of his cheerfulness by the time they reached the camp at Big Bar.

When the *Florence* came the next day he was made as comfortable as possible on borrowed air mattresses and entrusted to Kyle McGrady's care. By phone we directed an ambulance to meet the boat; and the compensation papers would go in at once. For Lark's wrenched back, medical science would have to do what it could.

And it did very well. When we saw Lark again, during the summer, he seemed as good as ever.

In our canyon the war was far away, although men were now being conscripted for a year of service in the United States Armed Forces, with service limited to the Western Hemisphere and the possessions of the United States. Our herders and farm help listened to their radios with some uncertainty, but not with fear. They had registered; they would be sent for when needed. Meanwhile some of them secretly wondered if they were passing up a big adventure by not enlisting.

Len sold our wool by phone and as usual handled the few fleeces Dick Carter always had to sell. Fifteen minutes later our wool would have brought five hundred dollars more, which was nothing to feel bad about, however. During World War I a sheepman friend of ours had been offered fifty-eight cents a pound, had held out confidently for sixty, and had finally sold for fifteen. What we had never had we could not lose—that was the best way to think about it, especially when we had done pretty well in any event.

One morning I rode the boat to Temperance Creek to see Hazel Johnson's new house. It was as modern as this morning's sun, but with all its wonders I regretted the passing of the old mixed-origins house of Anna's reign.

While *I* was having a delightful morning, Len was not. Everything had begun going bad. Bear had suddenly begun working on Mike's band. One walked coolly out of a timbered cover and snatched up a lamb, with Mike looking. The bear escaped, but it would certainly return. Another herder tied up the expensive bell-ewe Len had bought, using a rope around her neck. She had never been tied this way and strangled herself. Then one of our best dogs suddenly began to kill sheep.

"I can see," my distracted husband told me as I came in from my carefree wanderings, "how a sheepman can go nutty, but not paralyzed."

There was one piece of very good news, however. When I departed from the ranch with the children, some time in June, the house would not be left to bachelors and short-time women cooks. Al and Mrs. Reynolds had agreed to make their home at Kirkwood, and for the first time in his life Al would become a farmer. For my part, I had always thought of him as Ulysses, a man forever longing to get home, forever prevented.

Now seemed a good time for the Reynolds' to take a brief layoff, and they went out gaily. My crowd did not fall away much, yet school must hold a while for Pat and Steve. The latter finished with a jaunty flourish; and Pat completed her assignments and voluntarily took the state tests for the eighth grade. With the results of these I was quite contented.

When Len went out to bring Al and Jessie Reynolds back, he brought further good news. He had secured an option on a twenty-five acre tract that lay exactly as we had hoped, on a slope at the higher side of town. From this point we could look west to the Seven Devils and the blue Snake-Salmon wall, north over the checkered bedspread of Camas Prairie, east to the amethyst ranges beyond the Clearwater where our Pilot Rock camp had been, and south to the nameless foothills marking the edge of the Idaho wilderness. Here was the place for our stone house.

Rain was beginning, but every day I did a bit of packing, and meanwhile, rain or shine, Len started the sheep on trail. At Big Bar a precious crop of hay was down, and the men went there whenever the sun emerged for a few hours, and turned the wet shocks. Joe went too, doing whatever the men did, and taking care of his own horse.

My last week began. I had arranged by mail for an apartment in town, and now that lessons were done, the sheep on their way and the Reynolds' ready to take charge, my life in the canyon was about over.

The unceasing rain was giving me a bad time, this and the myriad small decisions that a move involves. As you sort and abandon clothing and letters, you sort and abandon old illusions. I would have liked my stay to end on a noble and triumphant note, but the insistent drumming of the rain, when at night I lay alone and wakeful, seemed to whisper trouble. I had survived a serious accident, circumvented the doctor's warning, and now maybe the canyon was preparing to block me with one last sly move.

Another dawn came, but it was too wet for the men to go up the river and presently the sullen sky sealed the canyon completely. Toward evening a faint light broke through the clouds, accompanied by an adverse breeze. Thankful for even this, and unable to bear the prisoning house any longer, I went down through the orchard in the dusk. I went to the farthest walnut tree; bigger than four ordinary trees its arms spread in lofty dignity. And now as I leaned against its pale trunk I wished I had put aside my work more often and come down here to lean and think, or just to lean.

Stars came out, and the Oregon wall took on a fine dramatic line. A bird, perhaps a mourning dove or a little owl, called insistently from over there, making itself heard, strangely, above the washing of the river across the submerged toes of Kirkwood Rock. In the shadow farther along our bar I could see the white blur of David Kirk's stone. Stars and wall, bird and river, Kirk and oblivion—I could derive no profounder meaning from all this than the knowledge that night was here and tomorrow another day.

By phone I engaged Lloyd Bash at Lucile to bring his truck to the end of the road above Till Phillips' on Friday about noon.

Tuesday began cool and clear, and when the ungracious sun at last emerged, the men went again to Big Bar to turn the hay. On their return Bob said sorrowfully, "That stuff up there's been turned so much it doesn't even look like hay any more."

On Thursday morning Al looked around outside and

came back to warn me. "You won't be leaving tomorrow. Even if it stops raining the summit will be too soggy to cross with loaded mules—they'd only bog down. You might as well resign yourself."

Al's counsel was rarely offered and never to be ignored. And when Celia Titus phoned to ask our plans, she agreed with Al. It was the wettest June she had ever seen on the river.

So I phoned Lloyd not to come until Saturday, but I wondered if someone would phone him on Saturday not to come at all.

On Friday morning the sun came out with specious promise, and though I did not trust it, I began putting the last things in the boxes and marking those that must go on the mules and setting aside those that could be sent out later.

Saturday dawned weak and deceitful, but I was resolved to get away before the rain could make up its mind. By eight we were ready, with three solidly packed mules and enough saddle-horses for everyone. Bob would go along to bring back the stock.

As we rounded the bend that would shut the house from view, I took no last look, and the children were not thinking about such a thing. Along the creek the wet trees sprinkled us as we brushed through, but the rain withheld; and after we started up Sumac Gulch the trails were almost dry. With not a single untoward happening and with increasingly bland skies, we reached the top.

At Dick Carter's no one was visible, and since the road now came above Till's we should not see him either. I was sorry, for both had been true and delightful friends.

I thought of others I should see again rarely if ever: the

Axtells, who had moved away; the Hibbses, the McGaffee families, the Tituses and Kenneth Johnsons; the Slim Johnsons, who had left Cow Creek for a remoter ranch on the divide; and especially I thought of Mr. Russell.

The canyon was dropping farther behind, and I could no longer see the Oregon rims, because of the pines through which we rode. The children and I were through with Snake River, and as soon as we could sell the ranch for what it was worth, Len would leave it too.

Our period in isolation had given the children resourcefulness, and put a color into their childhood that would be hard to buy—at least Len and I believed this. Also we were confident they could adjust themselves without great pain to public school and life in town.

Of course we, their parents, had taken the canyon adventure too seriously. But over-seriousness about work is not so much a fault as it is a stage. Our next adventure might be lighter in spirit, but it would have to be connected, as this one had been, with *producing* something. Of that we were both sure.

I wished that Len were with me now, not out on the trail, the unholy, exhausting trail to summer range. But the cards had not fallen that way. Ahead I could hear the children's cries of pleasure as the panorama of the Salmon began to open, disclosing the great sun-misty regions to the east.

And at the end of the road Lloyd's truck was waiting.